Clay Sculpting
for Digital Media

Clay Sculpting for Digital Media

Stephanie Reese

Upper Saddle River, New Jersey 07458

Publisher: Dave Garza
Director of Production and Manufacturing: Bruce Johnson
Acquisitions Editor: Elizabeth Sugg
Developmental Editor: Judy Casillo
Editorial Assistant: Lara Dugan
Managing Editor: Mary Carnis
Manufacturing Manager: Ed O'Dougherty
Production Liaison: Denise Brown
Production Editor: Inkwell Publishing Services
Interior Design and Composition: Inkwell Publishing Services
Art Director: Marianne Frasco
Cover Design Coordinator: Miguel Ortiz
Cover Art: Kevin Odhner
Printing and Binding: Banta Harrisonburg
Cover Printer: Banta Harrisonburg

Trademarks

Super Sculpey, Sculpey, Premo, Sculpey III, Super Flex are trademarks of Polyform Corp.

Cernit is a trademark of T + F KUNSTOFFE FÜR TECNIK UND FREIZEIT GMBH (Germany).

Fimo is a trademark of EBERHARD FABER G.M.B.H.

Paperclay is a trademark of CREATIVE PAPERCLAY COMPANY, INC.

MicroScribe 3D is a trademark of Immersion Human Interface Corporation.

Softimage is a trademark of Softimage Corporation.

Alias is a trademark of Alias | Wavefront, a division of Silicon Graphics Limited.

3D Studio MAX is a trademark of Autodesk, Inc.

Other products and company names mentioned herein may be the trademarks of their respective owners.

Prentice-Hall International (UK) Limited, *London*
Prentice-Hall of Australia Pty. Limited, *Sydney*
Prentice-Hall Canada Inc., *Toronto*
Prentice-Hall Hispanoamericana, S.A., *Mexico*
Prentice-Hall of India Private Limited, *New Delhi*
Prentice-Hall of Japan, Inc., *Tokyo*
Prentice-Hall Singapore Pte. Ltd.
Editora Prentice-Hall do Brasil, Ltda., *Rio de Janeiro*

10 9 8 7 6 5 4 3 2 1

ISBN 0-13-085246-5

Contents

Acknowledgments

A book is a collaborative effort by many, many people. I have tried to name everyone who had input into this process. If I've left anyone out, please accept my apologies.

First, I want to thank my husband, Andrew Reese; without his help, encouragement, and unlimited support, this book would never have been written.

Many thanks to Judy Casillo and Elizabeth Sugg, my editors at Prentice Hall, who were patient and believed in this project.

Special thanks go to Richard and Jodi Creager of the Creager Doll Studio; Konrad Dunton of Pacific Data Images; Richard Miller and Mark Siegel of Industrial Light & Magic; and Craig Hayes of Tippitt Studios, who all unselfishly shared their expertise and experience.

Thanks to Judy Conner at Pacific Data Images, who kept answering my phone calls, and who gave me permission to use their images and to talk with the master, Konrad Dunton.

Thanks to Nagissa Namoto for permission to use their images; and to Mark Anderson, model shop supervisor at Industrial Light & Magic, who allowed me to talk with their sculptors, Richard Miller and Mark Siegel.

Thanks to Cindy Chang at Universal Studios, who gave permission to use the *Dragonheart* photos.

Thanks to Rebecca Herrera at 20th Century Fox, for permission to use the *Jumanji* images.

Special thanks to Jan Sherman, Vice President of Creative Services for The Sally Corporation, who allowed me to use images of their wonderful animatronic armatures and characters.

Most of all I wish to thank all the talented students at The Art Institute of Phoenix, who allowed me to use their work for all to learn from.

I wish to thank the following companies and people who generously provided equipment, services, and software for the writing of this book: Paul Cirre, Eastman Kodak Co, for the use of their DC120 digital camera; it made images for this book possible. David Hague, Immersion Corporation, who answered my digitizing questions and allowed me to use a MicroScribe digitizing arm.

Thank you to the content experts who provided valuable comments and suggestions for this text in the course of its development: Scott F. Hall, SUNY Alfred State College; Robert King, ITT Technical Institute; Steve Missal, The Art Institute of Phoenix; James Mohler, Purdue University; Scott Nelowet, The Art Institute of Ft. Lauderdale; and Pierre Pepin, The Art Institute of Ft. Lauderdale.

Introduction

In the past, sculpting and puppet-making were used primarily in the entertainment industry as stop-motion animation or reference tools. That situation changed dramatically with the introduction of real-world sculpting as a technique for creating computer-generated dinosaurs for the movie *Jurassic Park*. The dinosaurs, created in clay and then duplicated on the computer using digitizing devices, gave animators entirely new freedom in character creation.

The good news is that this technique has opened up a new field for artists interested in character design and production. Artists who were previously confined to the limitations of their computer hardware and software for character design now have the freedom to use real-world techniques to create their characters in clay.

Clay Sculpting for Digital Media is designed for the beginning student as well as the advanced artist. It is structured in a step-by-step format to be read in the order presented. This provides the student continuity in the learning process and assures that he or she will complete an entire character by the end of the book.

The book is divided into seven chapters that reflect how I teach this course in the classroom.

Chapter 1 is an overview of the clays and tools used in the animation industry for character creation.

Chapter 2 covers planning the character design, including how to create concept drawings, model sheets, and schematic drawings. It also covers the types of armatures (or skeletons) used in animation models as well as in animatronics and stop-motion animation. Finally, it covers the different materials and techniques used for building bent wire armatures.

Chapter 3 takes a detour from the creation process to show the student how working sculptors produce characters. Interviews with professional character artists and sculptors from several animation houses give the student insights into their craft and a better understanding of how the parts all come together in later chapters.

Chapter 4 introduces the sculpting process. Step-by-step tutorials guide the student in creating a realistic human head.

Chapter 5 continues work on the head to include the anatomy of the neck and the addition of teeth, tongue, wrinkles, skin texture, and expressions.

In Chapter 6, students use what they learned in Chapter 2 to create an armature that fits the character. Sculpting of hands and body muscles is covered, as well as clothing creation, hair, and painting and finishing of the character.

Chapter 7 provides an overview of the digitizing process and describes how the student might expect to create sculptures for different methods.

I hope that you find this book helpful in creating your own character in clay. Enjoy and have fun.

Stephanie Reese

Clay Sculpting
for Digital Media

Chapter 1

Clay

Chapter Objectives

- Learn how clays are used in animation.
- Learn about the new clays.
- Learn to work with synthetic clays.
- Learn to cure synthetic clays.
- Learn which sculpting tools to use.

Historical Overview

Clay sculpting is certainly not new to filmmakers. Clay sculptures have been used for years to produce molds for creatures in stop-motion sequences. Classic stop-motion animators like Willis O'Brien and Ray Harryhausen brought fantasy to life in films such as *King Kong, Clash of the Titans, Seven Voyages of Sinbad,* and *Sinbad and the Eye of the Tiger.* Clay animators like Helena Smith Dayton (one of the first women clay animators), Art Clokey (creator of *Gumby*), and Will Vinton (known for coining the term *claymation,"* for the *California Raisons,* and for his work on the current television show *The PJ's*) raised the use of clay to the level of fine art. *Nightmare Before Christmas* was a full-length celebration of the art form, and even *Jurassic Park* was begun with miniatures and stop-motion (or go-motion) in mind. Through the phenomenal efforts of the Industrial Light & Magic computer team under Dennis Muren, the first realistic creature movement generated by computer became a reality.

With the increasing use of computer-generated animation in film and the development of more complex characters in interactive entertainment, character clay sculpting has become a talent much in demand today. Animators knocking on the doors of hot animation houses are being asked for examples of their "Sculpey work" in addition to their usual sample reels. It's not enough just to have Softimage, Alias, or 3D Studio MAX down pat; you need to be an artist and sculptor as well. Companies like Viewpoint in Utah are creating clay sculptures solely as a means to create computer mesh models for sale (e.g., the Dancing Baby seen on the sitcom *Ally McBeal*).

For those of you who have been working primarily in the computer realm, working in clay offers many rewards. Not only does it let you produce marvelously detailed creatures or characters, but the feel of actually manipulating the clay to form your creature is tactilely rewarding. Besides, you can't sit at a computer *all* the time! This approach offers the best of both worlds: the creativity of moving clay between your fingers to create something unique, and the ability to transfer your creation into the computer to bring it to life.

Typically there are three areas of computer animation in which clay finds a comfortable home: stop-motion, maquettes, and digitizing. We'll cover some of the special issues for each of these applications in later chapters. First, let's discuss the types of clay available for maquette and digitizing model construction.

Clays

There are hundreds of different types of clay available for every conceivable purpose. However, most are unacceptable for use with digitizers, stop-motion, or maquettes. Generally, clays can be categorized by the substances they're made from or how they're hardened.

Earth Clays

Earth clays are just that, clays made from the earth, such as terra cotta and porcelain. These clays are used primarily when the clay itself is the end product. While they *could* be used, they're not really right for this type of project. Earth clays must be kept damp while you're working on them or storing them, which means that you're constantly misting them while working, to fight their tendency to dry out. They must also be stored in plastic and kept cool.

Earth clays also require high-temperature firing, some up to 2400 degrees Fahrenheit. To achieve that temperature, you need a specialized kiln, a source of power, good quality ceramic tools for working with high-temperature objects, and the necessary space to let red-hot objects cool—not the best environment to share with computers. Earth clays are also fragile, which means that they sometimes explode during firing, crack while cooling, break easily when done, and are hard to repair without chips and cracks. All in all, earth clays are impractical for digitizing, stop-motion, or maquette construction.

Polymer Clays

My favorite clays to work with are categorized as synthetic or polymer clays, as shown in Figure 1-1.

Polymer clays have become popular in recent years for use on items that require a short working time. Although polymer clays don't have the surface quality of fine porcelain, they will withstand more abuse and some can be baked

Figure 1-1 *A variety of brands and types of polymer clays is shown. This image does not include all available choices. For information on where these clays can be purchased, see the Appendix.*

at low temperatures easily. Polymer clays were first developed in Germany in 1930. They are made from polyvinyl chloride (PVC). Here is a list of some popular synthetic clays used for sculpting:

- *Plastilina* (a.k.a. plasticene) is basically clay powder mixed with oil and wax instead of water, and comes in many varieties and hardness levels. You know it as that colored modeling clay you used as a kid. Plastilina can't be fired and doesn't dry out. It remains in its unbaked form; therefore, the softer types of plastilina must be refrigerated prior to digitizing. However, most types of plastilina that are used for digitizing are either rubber or rock hard when they're at room temperature. To use these for sculpting, the plastilina must be warmed to approximately 130 degrees to make it soft enough to manipulate. It can be warmed in the microwave in small batches, however, the best solution is to use a cheap bun warmer or warming tray so you have a steady supply of softened clay. When using plastilina for digitizing, a light touch is called for with the digitizing probe. A popular type of plastilina used in model making is Roma Plastilina #3 or #4. The numbering on Roma Plastilina represents the hardness level of the clay, #1 being the softest. Other types of plastilina are available, such as Wed Clay and Kleen Klay. Chavant, Inc. sells a wide variety of plastilina, which comes in many strengths, as seen in Figure 1-2.

- *Sculpey*, a white polymer clay from Polyform Products, is rougher in texture after firing. Its soft consistency makes it more difficult to sculpt with than some other polymer clays. Super Sculpey has generally replaced it.

- *Super Sculpey*, shown in Figure 1-3, has a pink skin tone, has a smoother texture than Sculpey, and is much easier to sculpt. It is the most popular clay for smaller maquettes. Also from Polyform Products, Super Sculpey is an oil-based clay that can be fired in a standard home oven at relatively low temperatures.

- *Sculpey III*, another Polyform Products clay, is similar to Super Sculpey but is usually sold in smaller quantities. It comes in a variety of colors, but beware of color bleeding. Like Super Sculpey, Sculpey III can be oven-fired.

Figure 1-2 *Plastilina is shown here in many varieties and strengths. The examples shown in plain wrappers are from Chavant, Inc. They are used for professional modeling that requires exact scaling and measurement (e.g., automobile design). The clay is available in several choices of surface hardness to give the modeler more control over the medium.*

Figure 1-3 *Super Sculpey is the polymer clay of choice by many artists because of its easy workability.*

- *ProMat* is stiffer and harder to work with than Super Sculpey, but it will bake harder and take more abuse. Many artists mix ProMat with Super Sculpey to get the best qualities of each.

- *Premo* is an additive clay that was introduced to the market in January 1998. Although it is intended to replace ProMat, it is not meant to be used on its own as ProMat was. Instead, Premo is meant to be mixed with Super Sculpey, either 1 part Premo to 1 part Super Sculpey or 1 part Premo to 2 parts Super Sculpey, to provide more strength and durability to the Super Sculpey clay. See Figure 1-4 for samples of Premo.

- *Fimo*, shown in Figure 1-5, a polymer- and oil-based clay from Eberhard Faber in Germany, is similar to Sculpey III. It's very crumbly and stiff right out of the package, but with sufficient handling, it's easier to work with than Sculpey III. Try Fimo after you have had some experience with other clays. Fimo is a firmer clay that will hold detail better than others. It is available in small packages of precolored clay, but because it's imported, it tends to be more expensive than other clays. Unlike Sculpey III, the colors have much less tendency to bleed.

- *Cernit* is manufactured by T+F GmbH, Dreieich, Germany. It can be either baked in an oven or boiled (yum!). Be careful when baking Cernit, however, because it has a tendency to burn; it also tends to surface-check over time. Cernit has a much more waxy appearance than other polymers. Although it comes in a light pink color, Cernit turns whitish on baking.

Figure 1-4 *Premo can be blended with Super Sculpey to make the clay more durable. It is available in a variety of colors.*

Figure 1-5 *Fimo is similar to Sculpey III in that it's available in many colors. It can be mixed with Super Sculpey to create tinted or more translucent skin.*

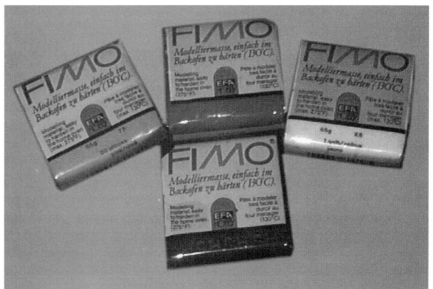

Other clays with new and interesting characteristics are coming onto the market all the time. Clays that can be water-hardened, oven-baked, and air-dried are manufactured to meet the rising demands of artists in all mediums.

Papier-Mache

Papier-mache "clays" work well in some instances. You can buy standard papier-mache-type mediums that are gray and grainy. However, a new hybrid has been developed that has a smoother and more clay-like texture while still giving you the flexibility of air-drying. Paperclay is the brand name for the most popular product of this type, created by the Creative Paperclay Company. Containing volcanic ash and paper pulp, it air-dries, requiring no firing in a kiln or oven. Paperclay, shown in Figure 1-6, is comparatively very light in weight and adheres easily to most surfaces. It's much smoother and easier to work with than standard papier-mache. The downside of Paperclay is that, like earth clays, it needs to be kept damp while sculpting and during storage.

Figure 1-6 *Paperclay is an alternative to Super Sculpey that can be air-dried. It can also be used in conjunction with Super Sculpey as a lightweight interior filler.*

A Paperclay sculpture dries from the outside in. This can result in a dry-to-the-touch feel on the outside while the clay is still wet on the inside. Unfortunately, if you attempt to paint or seal Paperclay before it is completely dry, it may mold. The good news about Paperclay is that it won't break or crack as easily as the polymer clays, and for this reason, it's good to use as the center structure of a body that would otherwise require lots of heavier clay.

Even though Paperclay is much smoother and easier to work with than standard papier-mache, when dried, the finish of Paperclay still resembles paper. Artists who use Paperclay for their final work usually sand the surface after drying. For a smoother, porcelain-like finish, you can apply coats of gesso (a paste typically made from whiting and size or glue applied to a surface before painting) before sanding. I recommend three coats to achieve a smooth surface. If you will be painting the figure for any reason, the gesso coating will provide a smoother surface. When you're done, always remember to seal the surface with a matte spray sealer.

Other air-dry clays are available that are not paper-based and are good for pattern-making, such as for a pouring mold or digitizing. These clays are not acceptable for a finished figure because as they dry, the surface tends to crack.

Sculpting with Polymer Clay

If you're used to working with earth clays, polymer clays take a little acclimating. Polymers are much more pliable and require a gentle touch—they move quite easily as you sculpt. The clay also softens with the heat of your hands, so sending it to the refrigerator periodically helps harden it up again if it gets too soft to work with easily.

When I first started using Super Sculpey, the formula was slightly different from that on the market at this writing. It was stiffer then and baked at a slightly higher temperature. This resulted in a stronger finished work. For whatever reasons, Polyform Products changed the formula and a softer, less efficient clay was the result. With this in mind, here are a few tips for working with Super Sculpey effectively:

- Super Sculpey can be sculpted like any earth clay. However, unlike earth clays, it doesn't require an armature that must be removed before the figure is fired.

- Polymer clays needn't be vented, or hollowed, as a typical earth-clay sculpture requires. Polymer clays don't explode during baking in a normal oven, but you must consider the thickness of clay you're baking so that it is baked all the way through. With this in mind, other, lighter substances can be substituted for the interior mass of the figure, such as aluminum foil, lightweight wood, urethane foam (not Styrofoam), wax, and even paper or papier-mache.

- Although Super Sculpey is generally easy to use, test the clay for softness when you buy. Clay that is too soft in the box can become gummy as you work.

- An artist used to earth clay will probably find polymer clay harder to control at first compared to the earth clay, because it moves around so much during working.

- When sculpting with polymer clay, remember that it is oil-based clay and will pick up any dirt or oil from your hands. The end result may resemble marble cake! This isn't a problem with a digitizing model, but it does look rather unappealing to the client.

- Another thing to keep in mind about polymer clay is that it eats into some plastics after awhile. Be careful not to use plastics for interior structures, long-term storage containers, or as a working surface. A glass working surface is far superior as it can be cleaned easily while helping to keep the clay free of dirt.

- When baking Super Sculpey or other polymer clays, any glass or metal pan can be used. However, a piece must be set up to avoid slumping as it bakes. If I'm going to bake a small head, say, 2 inches in height, I sculpt the head on an armature consisting of a wooden dowel or brass tube. (See chapter 4 for details of this procedure.) I then use a small wood block stand with a hole for the dowel or a wire that fits inside the tubing. See Figure 2-14, Chapter 2. This stand keeps the head upright while it's baking in the oven. If you don't have a stand or don't want a tube coming out of the head, lay the head down on a crumpled paper towel in a pan. This will at least keep it from rolling. You can use any material that won't burn or melt at low temperatures. (Paper burns at just over 450 degrees Fahrenheit.)

- When sculpting long parts such as arms and legs, you must have some type of armature inside to keep them straight and to take the weight off the clay. I recommend going to your local home improvement store and checking out the stock of bare, solid copper wire. It comes in a variety of sizes and is dirt cheap. The copper wire is sturdy and makes a very "dead" armature, meaning that it has very little springback.

• Another tip for sculpting long parts is to use a pattern cut from illustration board as a guide. Simply draw a front view and a side view as shown in Figure 1-7.

Figure 1-7 *The leg pattern has been drawn in both front and side views and the pattern has been cut out of illustration board.*

Cut the shapes out and make slits down the centerline of each: from the bottom up to the midpoint on the front view and from the top down to the midpoint on the side view, as shown in Figure 1-8.

Slide the two shapes together to form a three-dimensional form as shown in Figure 1-9. This form can be duplicated for however many legs, arms, tentacles, and so on your figure has. Now all the limbs will be the same size and shape. These patterns can be attached to the armature with epoxy or hot glue, and then clay can be added over the pattern as shown in Figure 1-10. Remember to cover the pattern with enough clay to keep it from cracking along the edges.

• Larger heads and parts require a larger oven and larger fixtures. You can also create your piece in sections and bake them individually. Once baked, assemble them using Super Sculpey as a filler to complete a larger digitizing model.

Warning: Never bake polymer clay in a microwave oven unless the manufacturer specifically approves the clay for microwave. Unless it is specifically formulated for microwave use (and I know of no such clays at this writing), polymer clay can explode, causing injury or death. Moreover, placing a metal armature in a microwave oven can cause electrical arcing and other serious and permanent problems.

Figure 1-8 *Slits have been cut from the bottom up to midpoint on the front and from top down to midpoint on the side so the pattern can be assembled in a three-dimensional model.*

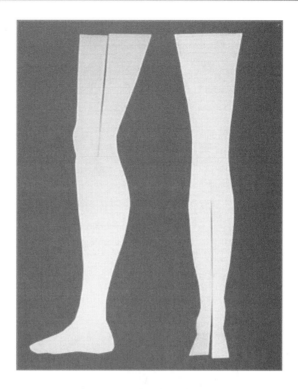

Figure 1-9 *The model is assembled and ready to apply to the leg armature.*

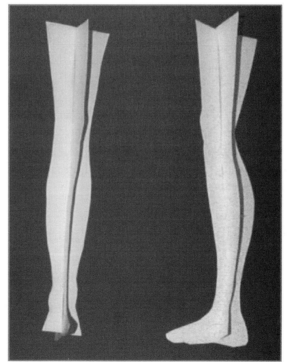

Kneading the Clay

Clays must be kneaded to make sure they are mixed well and softened sufficiently. Don't be fooled by clays that appear to be soft enough to sculpt without kneading. If you choose not to knead your clay, you might be disappointed by the results. Surface blemishes and brittleness can appear after baking and ruin

Figure 1-10 *The clay is applied over the paper pattern to form the leg.*

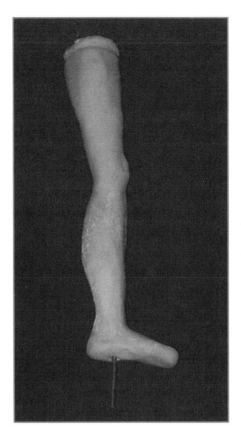

hours of work. While kneading will help you mix the clay and produce a better surface, it can also be harmful if you don't work the clay correctly. Air bubbles can form and be trapped in the clay as you're kneading. This can cause blemishes on the clay surface, or worse, cracking when the piece is baked. These methods should cut down the risk of producing air bubbles as you knead the clay:

1. After you have softened the clay, roll the clay flat and fold it over onto itself. Repeat until clay is mixed sufficiently.

2. After clay is softened, roll clay between your hands to form a long worm. Fold the worm in half and repeat the process until the clay is mixed thoroughly.

3. For softer clays, a pasta maker can be used to knead the clay. The clay must first be warmed enough to be pliable. (If it's not pliable, wrap it in a towel and put it on a heating pad.) Then it can be cut into chunks and fed through the machine on its widest setting. If the clay isn't soft enough before being fed through the machine, it will simply shred.

Note: Don't use the family pasta maker to knead or split your polymer clay. Once you have used it for polymer clay, it is no longer safe for foodstuffs.

Once the clay has been kneaded, it doesn't have to be rekneaded if you must wait before using it. Simply wrap the clay in paper towels and put it on a shelf for storage.

Mixing Clays

There's a little bit of chemist in all of us. We want to mix clays with different characteristics together in an attempt to get that perfect medium. My recommendation is not to do this. The only exception is mixing clays from the same manufacturer (as with Super Sculpey and ProMat or Premo). The hazard of mixing clays with other clays or with paints is possible incompatibility, which might cause unexpected or undesirable results. Many artists I know mix Fimo or Cernit with Super Sculpey to produce a more translucent look, as well as a stiffer medium. However, reports of crumbling figures and surface checking are reasons to perform these experiments only when time isn't a factor.

Tools

Sculpting tools for polymer clays are really a matter of personal choice. In my extensive selection of high-tech sculpting tools, as shown in Figure 1-11, I have everything from fine dental tools and wire sculpting tools to plain old orange sticks.

Figure 1-11 *A variety of really nifty tools.*

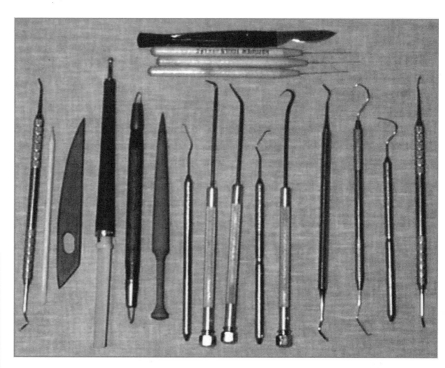

TIP

USING DENTAL TOOLS

If you like dental tools—and there are some that are really nice for some uses, such as the dental spoons shown in Figure 1-12—ask your dentist for discards. They can be useless to him or her and still be very handy for you.

Even with all of these tools available, I prefer the orange sticks. Orange sticks can be found in any beauty supply store or as cuticle tools in a nail kit. An orange stick is a smooth, wooden stick with a rounded point on one end and a flattened slice on the other, as shown in Figure 1-12. This tool lets me get into small areas such as around the eyes without creating holes, as can happen with sharp dental tools.

For larger sculptures, I buy a piece of $3/_{16}$-inch or $1/_{4}$-inch wood dowel and sand it at an angle to make a larger version of an orange stick. An X-acto knife

Figure 1-12 *Orange sticks, shown here to the left, are my high-tech tools of choice. However, dental spoons, like the flattened, rounded tool second from the right, also have nice, rounded shapes that are small enough to get into tight places without making holes in your clay.*

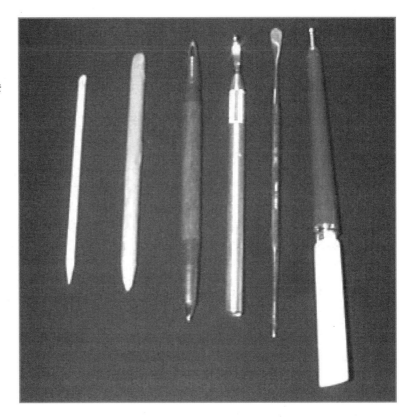

with a #11 blade is also vital for making precise cuts through the clay, for separating fingers and such. The other important tool I use all the time is a $\frac{1}{4}$- to $\frac{1}{2}$-inch-wide flat paintbrush. This helps me smooth areas of a face that I can't get to with my fingertip.

The last, and probably most effective, tools I use, are my hands. You just don't have the same feel working on a clay piece exclusively with tools. I have to hold it in my hand first and use my fingers until I need the tools for fine detail work. It's as if the creature you are creating is being born as you work.

Smoothing the Clay

The question I'm asked most often by other sculptors is how to get polymer clay smooth. This can be a tricky feat with polymer clays because they are so malleable. For example, you can be holding a polymer clay object tightly while you smooth it, when suddenly, it's distorted to one side from the tightness of your grip. Here are some ways to smooth the clay and prevent distortion, both before and after baking.

Before Baking

- Use wire sculpting tools to remove clay from an object without disturbing the surrounding clay. These tools are made of a wire loop embedded in a wooden handle. If you can't find wire tools the size you need, you can easily make them with wire, a wooden dowel, and some epoxy glue. In a pinch, I've also used plastic credit cards for smoothing low-detail areas such as the backs of heads.

- A mixture of acetone-based fingernail polish remover and a small amount of light vegetable or mineral oil, or straight acetone, will smooth polymer clays. It works by breaking down the clay enough to smooth the surface. Rub just a small amount onto the surface of the piece. However, be careful that you don't use too much of this magic elixir; the clay will start to become sticky and you can smooth away all the detail. (A diluent marketed by Polyform Products will also smooth and soften the clay. It is basically an oil that can be added to the clay. I don't recommend this; in my experience, it makes the clay too soft and sticky to work with.) See Figure 1-13.

Figure 1-13 *Elixirs used to smooth polymer clays, such as acetone-based fingernail polish remover and Sculpey Diluent, are shown here with Krylon Matte Finish #1311, used as a sealer for most projects.*

- Another resource, one that might not sound particularly attractive or sanitary but does indeed work, is saliva. Yep, regular spit does the job as well as anything. The salts in the saliva work on the clay to break it down, like the acetone. I use this especially in small figures or anything I'm sculpting for a fine-art piece, because I haven't determined for myself whether acetone-treated clay stands up over the long haul. Spit does; don't ask me why. However, if the objects are to be used for molds or digitizing, life expectancy usually isn't a significant factor. Most movie props and models seldom last much past a single use, anyway.

Note: I have no idea whether there is a health hazard from using saliva on models that will be handled by more than one person. I doubt it, both because of the inhospitable clay environment and the oven baking temperature. However, sensible health precautions seem to be in order here: There are potential risks from contact with human fluids. Be aware and be careful how you handle unbaked pieces.

> ### TIP
>
> ## BURNISHING SYNTHETIC CLAY
>
> If you must have a perfectly smooth surface, polymer clays can be burnished with smooth stones, just like earth clays. The best method I've found is to place the unbaked polymer clay sculpt in a freezer for 15 to 20 minutes until moisture condenses on the surface. Then use the stone to rub a shiny finish. I have acquired several burnishing stones over the years from rock shops and from other artists. They vary in shape and size, so I have a stone for any tight spot. Make sure there are no blemishes or flaws on the stone surface that will scratch the clay surface you're trying to smooth.

Note: With this method, the clay must be burnished entirely in one sitting. You can't refreeze the clay without losing the burnished surface you've already worked on.

After Baking

Even after a piece is smoothed completely, it will be somewhat rougher after it's fired. Many times what looked like a perfectly smooth finish before firing becomes noticeably bumpy afterward. This can become a problem when drawing grid lines on the surface of an object. Here are some guidelines to follow:

- After baking, smoothing can best be accomplished by sanding. After the piece is fired, I recommend using wet-dry sandpaper and lava soap. Sand the piece under running water. For removing lumps and bumps, 400-grit sandpaper works well. Be sure not to sand too heavily or you'll end up with a flat spot where your bump was before. For surface smoothing and polishing, use 600-grit sandpaper. If the bumps are really large, use an X-acto knife to trim away the excess. It's a little like performing outpatient surgery.

Baking

Baking the clay piece can sometimes be a trick in itself. Horror stories abound from anyone who has worked with polymer clays. The good news is that, unlike earth clays, almost anything is fixable with polymers. The techniques for baking polymers vary from artist to artist. Some are extremely careful about the exact time and temperature and cooling the piece ever so carefully in the oven, while others have sworn allegiance to their own methods of taking a piece directly out of a hot oven and cooling it down in the freezer. That said, it should be apparent to you that there are no here are hard-and-fast rules. However, follow these guidelines when seeking the "perfect" baking method for you:

- When baking polymer clay, set the piece on a crumpled paper towel or use the armature or sculpting stand to bake the piece in an upright position. If your clay sculpture is laid flat against the baking surface, the clay will deform in the heat before it hardens. It can be a big disappointment when the sculpture you've worked on so diligently suddenly has a drooping arm or a flat head.

- Polymer clays must bake until the interior temperature is 265 degrees Fahrenheit. If it isn't cooked long enough, the clay will crumble and crack.

- Cracking can also occur if the clay is baked at too high a temperature. The maximum recommended temperature is 275 degrees Fahrenheit.

  Note: If you use too high a temperature, polymer clay also releases toxic fumes. For this reason, I strongly recommend keeping the area well ventilated and using an oven that isn't used for food preparation.

- Cracking usually occurs during the cooldown period after the piece is baked. I have tried every solution I've ever heard and have had the best results with leaving the piece in the oven to cool. Turn the oven off and open the door slightly to allow the piece to cool slowly.

Rebaking Polymer Clays

Polymer clays allow you the flexibility to change or add to your sculpture even after the sculpture has been baked. The hardened clay can be carved or cut to remove unwanted sections, and then fresh clay can be added, smoothed, and baked again. This works for everything from a clay sculpture that needs a nose job to a cracked sculpture that needs major repair.

> **TIP**
>
> **MENDING CRACKS**
>
> If cracks occur that are wide enough to move together when you press them with your fingers, glue with an instant cyanoacrylic glue, such as Super Glue, before adding clay over the crack to rebake.

> **TIP**
>
> In a pinch, even a hair dryer produces enough heat to bake clay sufficiently for repairs.

Temperatures remain the same for the second baking, but times can be reduced significantly so cracking won't reoccur.

After you add clay onto a previously baked sculpture, use a brush and your chosen smoothing medium to smooth the area where the new clay comes together with the previously baked clay. This will ensure that seams won't be visible on the finished sculpture.

Hazards of Polymer Clays

Like any artist working with new materials, you should be aware that some synthetic clay might contain toxic or hazardous chemicals. Although most clays sold in this country have been tested, precautions and directions for use must be followed precisely to safeguard yourself and those around you.

Chemical exposures may be cumulative, meaning that chemicals entering the body aren't flushed out and larger amounts may accumulate in the body. An advertisement of "nontoxic" on the label only tells you that the product passed the short-term, acute toxicity test specified by the Federal Hazardous Substance Act. Therefore, toxicity as a result of long-term exposure is still a possibility with products carrying a "nontoxic" label. The three ways you can be exposed to these chemicals are:

1. Dermal exposure, or through the skin, is probably a low risk with polymer clays; but if you show signs of dermatitis, discontinue use.

2. Inhalation exposure is more of a threat when using the polymer clays. Always work in a well-ventilated area. As already mentioned, polymer clay releases toxic fumes if fired at too high a temperature.

3. Ingestion may not seem a likely problem; after all, you're not planning to eat the clay like that Play-Doh you ate as a preschooler. However, ingestion can occur if contaminated utensils, pans, or even cooking surfaces used to work or bake the clay are later used for food preparation. Once used in the studio, never use an object as a food container or utensil. Even though it appears clean, the surface may be porous and may contain hazardous residuals that can migrate into foods.

Here are a few more health warnings to keep in mind:

- Never use a baked polymer clay object as a container for foods or tobacco.
- Be sure to wash your hands after handling the clays. Having polymer clay on your hands is an innocent way to transmit harmful chemicals into your system; the clays appear much cleaner while working with them than other mediums do.
- Keep all children (born and unborn) and animals out of the working area. They can be susceptible to risk from smaller levels of exposure.
- Ventilation is essential when firing polymer clays. A simple fan might not be enough to remove toxic vapors from the area. Make sure there is a good source for outside ventilation as well.

These warnings must also be heeded for other substances you will be using in the studio. Harmful chemicals can be found in adhesives, dyes, and paints, as well as thinners, solders, and resins. Aside from these more obvious examples, dust from woodworking, earth clays, plasters, and gypsum used for molds and fibers can also be dangerous to your health.

If you have questions about the safety of the product you're using, contact the manufacturer for a Material Safety Data Sheet (MSDS). If the manufacturer refuses to supply you with one, change brands.

For more information on art safety, contact these resources:

- College, University, and School Safety Council of Ontario, Workers Compensation Board, 80 Bloor Street, West, Suite 604, Toronto, Ontario, M5S2V1. Phone (416) 965-8726. Publisher of *A Personal Risk Assessment for Craftsmen and Artists.*
- Art Hazards Information Center, Center for Safety in the Arts, 5 Beeksman Street, Suite 1030, New York, NY 10038. Publisher of *Art Hazards News,* four pages, 10 issues per year. The Center also offers workshops on art safety regularly.
- Foundation for the Community of Artists (FCA), 280 Broadway, Room 412, New York, NY 10007. Publisher of *Artist Update,* containing information on resources, referrals, and group health insurance.

In Conclusion

It's always best to know your project and have a firm understanding of how your sculpture will be used before you choose the clay for your figure. Whether you're creating for stop-motion, maquettes, or a model for digitizing, using the right clay will make a project easier and faster. A plasticine clay might work well for stop-motion or really large pieces that are harder to bake. But if you can cut a figure into workable sections or are sculpting smaller figures for maquettes or digitizing, polymer clays are useful, workable clays. With them, you needn't worry about denting or about the surface softening while you are digitizing.

In the Next Chapter

In Chapter 2, you'll learn basic proportions for your figure, whether it's human, animal, or fantasy. We'll also cover the fundamentals of armature construction and present the step-by-step creation of a simple bent-wire armature.

Chapter 2

Body Design and Armature Basics

Chapter Objectives

- Learn to plan a character.
- Learn to assess body proportions.
- Learn to build armatures and stands.

In Chapter 1 we learned about the various clays available for use in making maquettes and digitizing models. In this chapter we look at planning a character and creating an armature to fit it.

Planning and Body Design

Designing the basic body shape is the first step in creating a character. You might be working from sketches—your own or someone else's—or just free-forming with a lump of clay in your hands. Whichever you're doing, you should first have an idea in mind of your target. Even if you're free-forming, you should have the needs or desires of the client in mind. This is also true if you're only doing a head. It still must attach to a body, so you'd better keep that vital connection in mind.

If your ultimate characters are going to be cartoonlike or alien, retaining some basis in reality is still vital. Your audience will better understand the character if they're not also trying to determine where to look on the character's "face" to see where it's looking and talking. That's why even aliens from the furthest reaches of the universe are depicted as basically anthropoid, with binocular vision and some sort of mouth-like orifice. The audience can appreciate the beastliness and otherworldliness of the character without losing the plot.

In addition, exaggeration used in cartooning and cartoonlike character animation to emphasize story elements and create humor is most effective if you have a good beginning from which to exaggerate. For example, it's harder for Droopy to drop his already sagging jowls in disappointment, but the same jowls would make him a wonderful subject for the exaggerated facial contortions caused by a roller-coaster ride.

Finally, retaining realistic underpinnings lets you worry more about story and character and less about the physics of a strange world where things just don't work as they do here. However, if the decision has been made to create a gravity-less world, for example, you must plan your character as if it evolved and lives in that environment.

You must also consider the aerodynamics or hydrodynamics of the body to create a believable character. If your creature must fly or swim, the shape of the body and wings or fins must be such that they all work within the physical system. Examine the shapes and weights of birds and fish in relation to their real-world environments, then mimic them for believability in the alternative world's environment. If, for instance, the air in a fantasy world is twice as thick as on earth, the same bird body could be supported by wings half as large. Think about it: If you want a more reptile-like flier, the body muscle and wing shape must be equally well designed to keep the creature in the air.

Land creatures have less need for a tapered form. They can walk on two, four, or as many legs as you want—or slither, jump, hop, roll, or use any other form of propulsion. Be sure to consider the means of movement when designing a character.

Maybe you'd like your creature to have more than one head—or no head at all, just eyes in the middle of his belly.

The bottom line is that if you're creating a character, you must consider the physics of its home world and include some way for it to sense and interact with its environment, communicate, emote, ingest energy, reproduce, and move. Determine how alien or "real"—that is, *human*—the character should be.

For a human character, consider the age, sex, race, color, and any special circumstances, such as disabilities, athletic prowess, and so on. The face and body of an NBA center will be quite different from that of an infant or a computer hacker. Be sure to consider all of these factors before you start to sculpt.

Observations on Human Form

The differences between the sexes have to be considered when you are modeling. The first area to look at is the human form.

Adult

In adult humans, other than the more obvious differences, men are usually taller, have wider shoulders, and narrower hips, and tend to have more body muscle than women. Women tend to be smaller in stature, with wider hips and narrower shoulders, and have a smoother, rounder appearance. As with any rule, there are many exceptions.

Here are some simple measurements to remember:

- The male form usually has wider shoulders (2 head *lengths*) as opposed to the female form (2 head *widths* wide).
- The male form has narrower hips (2 head widths) as opposed to the female form (2¹/₂ head widths).
- If you want to make the female figure shorter, the length will usually come off the thighs (up to ¹/₂ head) as well as the upper arm (up to ¹/₃ head).
- The elbow is usually just above the waist. (Remember that ape look!)
- The wrist is at the crotch.
- The head and torso is usually ¹/₂ the body length.
- The hand at the longest point is the same length as the chin to mid-forehead.
- The forearm from inside the elbow to the wrist is the same length as the foot.
- The head is usually 5 eye-widths wide.

Child

The body of a child is proportioned differently from the body of an adult. The geometric center, or the approximate midpoint in height, of an infant's body is near the navel until approximately age two, while an adult's geometric center is at the pubic bone. An adult's legs are thus roughly equal in length to the distance between the pubic bone and the top of the head. Because the infant does not use its legs for locomotion or weight carriage, they represent a much smaller proportion of its total length.

An infant's head is usually one-half the length of an average adult's head; by the time a child is six years old, the child's head size has grown to approximately three-fourths the length of an average adult head.

Here are approximate heights of children at different ages in head lengths;

- Infant—approximately four head-lengths in length, or one-fourth of an adult's height.
- Age three—5 HL and stands one-half of an average adult's height.
- Age six—6 HL tall.
- Age ten—6¹/₂ HL tall, or three-fourths the size of an average adult. Also, approximately as tall as the center of the adult chest.
- Age 16—Seven heads high and has usually reached his or her adult height.
- Age 20—Has reached adult height (7¹/₂ to 8 HL) and full stature is attained.

Older Characters (The Silver Foxes)

As humans age, several processes occur. The spine compresses and shortens as the vertebral disks degenerate and thin out. Osteoporosis and other diseases associated with aging can also cause the bones themselves to compress, especially in the vertebrae. The spine then assumes a more pronounced curvature, producing a hunched appearance as shown in Figure 2.1.

Figure 2-1 *With aging, the disks in the spine—and sometimes the vertebrae themselves—compress, producing a more pronounced curvature. Depending on the extent of these processes, a person can lose between one-half and one full head-length in height.*

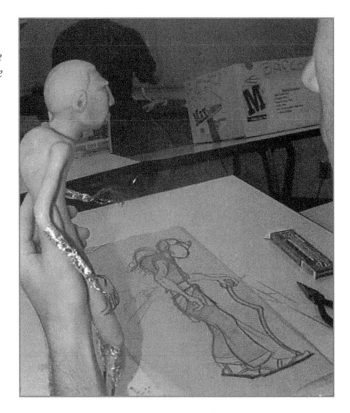

As the curvature increases with age, the neck appears to sink into the chest. As a result of these processes, some elderly people lose between one-half and one full head-length in height. These changes also produce a frail appearance.

Fantasy Characters

When creating fantasy characters, remember that there are "types" that we associate with different character personalities. Whether it's a hero, a villain, a bully, or a cute cuddly character, each type has a classic proportioned body type that has been developed by generations of cartoonists. To "sell" the idea that one of your creatures is heroic, villainous, or cute, borrow the appropriate form from previous animators who have preconditioned us to accept the appearance of each type.

Cute

If cute is what you need, your creature should have the same attributes as a baby. Generally, the cute character has an oversized head with large eyes. Its body is chubby and round.

Heroes

The male hero is displayed as the Superman image, triangular in body shape with a square chin. He should be very handsome, of course, in a cartoon sort of way.

The female heroine is displayed with an idealized conception of cartoon beauty. She is, after all, a characture of the "perfect" woman. She should have an exaggerated version of the traditional hourglass figure with long legs, small waist, and large breasts. The new wave of heroines seem much more muscular as well.

Villains and Other Bad Guys

To create a character who looks like a villain, use a more angular appearance. Think of Jafar in Disney's Aladdin, Rasputin in Fox Animation's Anastasia, or the evil queen in Sleeping Beauty. A villain's eyebrows are usually turned up at a 45-degree angle. The eyes are narrow. The face may also be angled to a pointy chin.

Fantasy villains can also be animals, anything from a rat (Professor Ratigan) to a tiger (Shere Khan). Obviously, a fuzzy bunny is never going to look like a villain.

The Bully

The bully is another type of villian who, instead of a long, angular face, usually has a small head on a large muscular or rotund body. Disney's giant in the classic cartoon *The Brave Little Tailor* is a typical cartoon bully. And who can think about bullies without mentioning Popeye's nemesis, Bluto?

Goofy Creatures

The goofy creature is the bumbler, the uncoordinated fool. This type of character is usually tall with large feet. The facial features are exaggerated, with a long face and neck.

Animal Characters

Whether your character is a four-legged animal that walks on all fours or a two-legged ape that walks and talks like a human, you will need some basic guidelines when creating an animal character.

Four-Legged

The basic quadruped structure is similar to a bridge. The vertebrae or spine acts as the bridge span and is supported in the front and back by columns. These columns are made up of the shoulders and legs in the front and the pelvis and legs in the rear. The skeletal structure is secured in the front by muscles in the neck and in the rear by muscles in the hindquarters. The pelvis sits on a downward slant. As the rear legs are straightened, this body type helps move weight-bearing to the vertebrae without losing power.

Although both the pelvis and shoulders support the weight of the animal, the front legs and shoulders support most of the body weight, roughly two-thirds. The other one-third of the body's weight is supported by the rear quarters.

Neck and head movement between the shoulders and chest is aided by a pivotal point on the shoulder blade that works like a counterweight on a crane. This is best typified by the up-and-down head movement of a horse as it walks.

Although these basic structural principles apply to any four-legged animal, quadrupeds differ significantly in detail, beginning with their proportions. Examine an animal's proportions to learn how its body functions. For example, the giraffe is constructed so that it can graze in the tops of trees, while the cow gets its food from ground level. The giraffe gains most of its moisture from the foliage it eats; its long neck and legs make it quite difficult to drink from a ground-level pond. The cow, on the other hand, has a relatively short neck and legs that make it easy for the animal to drink from ground level. If the character you are creating is a combination of these animals, or part animal and part human, study how each piece will go together so you can construct an armature that will hold the bulk of the whole body.

Two-Legged

The ape family includes the only animals that walk in an upright (or at least semiupright) position. The gorillas, apes, and monkeys are used many times as the basis for a character. Things to consider when using an ape body type are:

- The ape thorax has a squarer shape than a human's; the shape only allows them to walk in a semiupright position.
- The ape still uses its forearms to assist in locomotion most of the time.
- Apes have arm and leg lengths just the reverse of ours. When they are on all fours, they have a downward slope from their heads to their pelvises, allowing them to be in a natural position for locomotion and to see all areas ahead of them as well.
- Because apes' legs are short and their arms and hands long, they can use their bodies as pendulums as they grip, climb, hang, and swing.
- The arm span of an average adult gorilla is 8 feet. A gorilla's thumb and big toe each oppose the other digits, allowing them to grasp and manipulate objects with either hand or foot.
- Short legs help the ape brace itself when climbing, while its large (11 inches long and 6 inches wide) feet help to support its 400-pound-plus weight on the ground.
- Although the body of a gorilla is shorter, it is also much more dense than a human's.

Some things to remember when sculpting a gorilla are:

- The pelvis is nearly twice as wide and twice as long as that of a human.
- The chest is at least one-fourth larger than a human's in both width and length.
- Gorillas have a pot-bellied appearance because of the mass of intestines needed to accommodate and digest its bulky diet.
- The female gorilla is shorter than the adult male and weighs only about half as much. Adult females average 4 1/2 feet tall and weigh just under 200

pounds. Average adult males are 5 to 5 1/2 feet tall and weigh roughly 450 pounds.

- The head of a gorilla is massive, with a bony sagittal crest on top and a bulging forehead that overhangs the eyes. The sagittal crest is especially apparent in males and provides an anchor for the large jaw muscles.

Now that you have a good idea about the type of character you need and what body characteristics it will have, the next step is to draw model sheets and schematics of your character to follow while sculpting.

Model Sheets and Schematics

A character plan that lists all the character's attributes that were discussed in the first part of this chapter provides a guideline to start drawing what your character will look like.

Concept Drawings

Concept drawings are free-form drawings that allow you to draw ideas about the look of your character. Maybe you have many ideas. Putting them on paper lets you choose which concept most closely fits your character's personality and body type. After a concept drawing has been chosen and refined to show the character you will sculpt, model sheets are in order.

Model Sheets

Traditionally, model sheets have been used to give animators a guideline to follow when animating specific characters. They show several views and personality shots, so that many animators can work on the same character while keeping the character's look and movement the same for every scene.

For sculpting maquettes, we'll use model sheets as a way to lay down a visual reference of your character. Different from a concept drawing, a model sheet shows more of the character's personality. The model sheet shows the character from several vantage points instead of only from a front view, and it includes some expressive poses—mad, angry, happy, sad, and so on—that suggest the character's personality. These poses can show whether the character is a shy Casanova or a devilish trickster. Head shots of the character are also added, to show facial expressions common to the character.

After concept drawings and model sheets have been drawn for your character, you're ready to draw a character schematic.

Character Schematic

Whether you're using a human model or an exaggerated fantasy figure, a schematic drawing can save you time and frustration. It provides drawn-to-size front and side views of your character, displaying all its physical characteristics. The schematic plays an important role in laying out and creating the armature, and sculpting the musculature, of your character. Each bend or twist of the character's body is shown, so that you can lay the armature wire directly over the image and bend it to the exact dimensions and angle of your character's form without extensive measuring.

Once the schematic drawings are complete, you're ready to start building the armature.

Armatures

Armatures are the bones and the basic structure of the sculpture. In figures for which synthetic clays are used, the armature will stay embedded in the piece even after firing, to hold the weight and keep the form of the character. This may seem odd to those of you who have used earth clays, for which the armatures are removed from the piece before firing.

In my character figures, I use brass, bronze, and copper to create the armatures; they don't discolor the clay as other metals do. These metals also have qualities that allow the armatures to function appropriately for the figure type. For example, if the character I'm creating has a lightweight body, I might use bronze rod and ball joints that can be locked into place, as seen in Figure 2.2. They keep the size of my work consistent and let me stand my work upright without any additional fixtures. In these less heavily weighted figures, the length of the armature continues down through the figure's feet and into a base to hold it upright. In figures with more body weight, it's useful to have a heavier armature so that the figure can stand on its own. (See the next section, Creating a Bent-Wire Armature.)

Figure 2-2 *The wire armature is complete with ball joints that can be locked into static positions.*

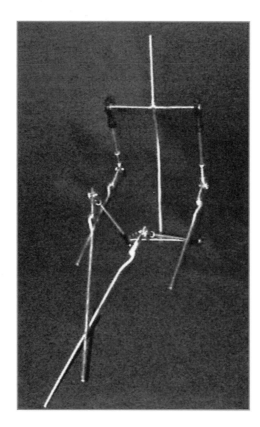

Note: Many would-be artists start out by using plastilina over plastic GI Joe dolls to build their characters. Plastic skulls, wooden skeletons—you name it, it's been tried. If you feel the urge to use something of this nature as a base for your creature, check out the hazards first, especially if you're using polymer clays that will be fired.

For heavier characters, the same materials can be used, only in larger diameters. Sometimes even characters with heavier bodies can be fitted with lighter-weight armatures with a little modification. The areas of the armatures that give under pressure on these wire wonders are the ball joints on the hips. A length of larger diameter wire is bent to fit along the hip and down one leg. It's secured with wire and soldered in place with silver solder. If the character will be placed in an action pose, leaving most of it's weight on one foot, an additional piece of $1/8$-inch brass square tubing, found at any hobby shop, is similarly secured along the side of the leg. The aluminum foil base and clay are applied over the wire, leaving only the opening of the tubing exposed at the bottom of the foot. Note that for this technique, the wire legs of the armature don't go through the feet into the base, as the lighter-weight character's did. Rather, the wire and tubing are cut off at the base of the feet so a wire attached to the base can be fed into the square tubing in the figure's foot. This puts the weight of the heavy figure on the wire armature instead of on the surrounding clay, eliminating cracking and breakage of the figure's legs.

Not every figure needs to have an armature with ball joints and complex construction. Most stationary figures use a simple bent-wire armature.

Creating a Bent-Wire Armature

Basic bent-wire armatures are typically used for maquettes that don't require motion in the joints, as shown in Figure 2-3. In these applications, wire is bent in the shape of a stick figure that matches the basic body shape of your creature.

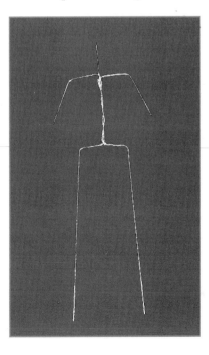

Figure 2-3 *The simple bent-wire armature shown can be used for static models. Wooden dowels used in the construction of the head can be attached to the wire neck. (See Chapter 6.)*

Lengths of brass tubing can sometimes be applied over the wire so that the tubing meets at either side of a joint. The tubing stiffens the structure and ensures that the structure will bend precisely at the joint line every time.

For heavier characters, heavy (#6) solid copper wire, as shown in Figure 2-4, is used for the torso, arms, and legs.

Figure 2-4 *Heavy #6 solid copper wire is used for the torso, arms, and legs of the armature.*

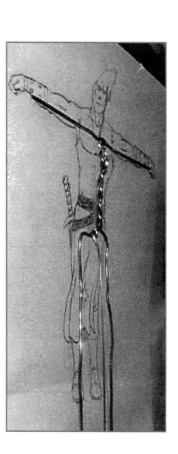

TIP

USING LEAD WIRE

If you use lead wire in a bent-wire armature, apply shrink or latex tubing over the lead so it doesn't come into contact with your skin. (Lead is poisonous, after all.)

Copper wire tends to be more "dead" than brass or bronze and is heavy enough to hold the weight. The neck and any other appendages—tails, ears, and so on—are created with $3/32$-inch bronze brazing rod. This is a good choice for short lengths, or for those areas that don't need to hold a lot of weight. The character heads are sculpted on a wooden dowel (see Chapter 4) that can be drilled to take the narrow neck wire; that makes this "Mr. Potato Head" method of sculpting easier to assemble.

The first step in making a simple bent-wire armature is to know the size and shape of your character (refer to schematic and model sheets earlier in this chapter). Since most bodies, whether they are realistic or fantasy, are measured in head size, a good first step is to have the character's head sculpted, as in Chapter 4. However, if you want to start with an armature first, know the head size you will sculpt so you can measure accordingly. Then work to keep the head size correct when you get to that stage.

Now let's make a simple bent-wire armature.

1. Lay wire over the scaled drawing of the character to measure the lengths of arms, shoulders, spine, and so on.

2. Using heavy-duty pliers, bend #6 solid copper wire to include arm length and shoulder for both sides of the body, as seen in Figure 2-5. (Two pairs of pliers are recommended so you can hold the wire with one pair as you bend with the other.)

Figure 2-5 *Wire is bent to form the arms and shoulders for both sides of the body.*

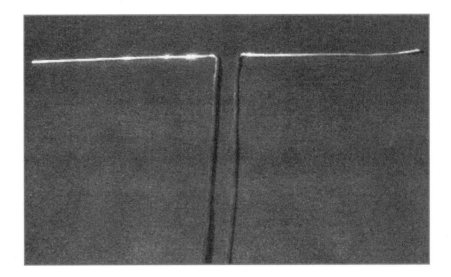

3. Holding the shoulder ends of both pieces of wire in position with spine toward the center, twist the wires around each other to twist together the spine section of the armature, as shown in Figure 2-6 a.

Figure 2-6 a *The two sides are held together to twist the spine together.*

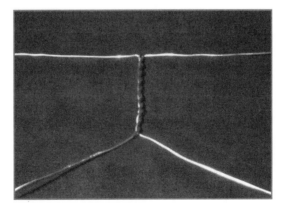

4. Bend the wire to include shoulders and hips, forming the body shape to match the shape of your character as shown in Figure 2-6 b.

Figure 2-6 b *The figure has been bent to match the body shape. Note that the spine has been bent to form the curve of the back.*

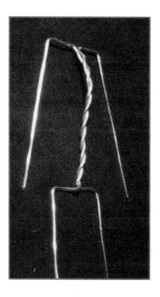

Now let's add the neck wire.

1. Cut the $3/32$-inch bronze brazing rod 4 to 5 inches long. This is much longer than we need; however, the rod is much easier to bend in a longer length, and we'll cut it to length later.

2. Twist the brazing rod through the spine twist and bend it around the spine securely, leaving a length of rod long enough to come up from the center of the spine into the wooden dowel in the character's head, as shown in Figure 2-7.

If the brazing rod still seems loose, wrap 20-gauge floral wire in a figure eight pattern around the shoulders and neck, as shown in Figure 2-7.

Other appendages such as tails can be added at this point in the same way.

Figure 2-7 *The neck wire is wound through the spine and bent up to provide a neck for the armature.*

For characters that don't have human characteristics (a four-legged animal or insect, for example), the same type of armature can be used. For this type of armature, having a detailed drawing or schematic of what the character will look like is also essential. The body is still produced with two lengths of heavy-gauge wire and twisted together along the spine, but the body and legs are bent to match the body of your character.

Characters with features that protrude from the body, like wings, antennae, tails, and so on, need extra support in those areas. Adding wire to the base skeleton can ensure that the weight of the clay won't snap the appendage off the body. Sometimes all that's needed is an extra extension of wire. But a more complex shaped extension, made with wrapped wire to form a cage, helps not only to hold up the part, but to shape it as well. This is great for ears or flying capes or anything that needs form.

Other Types of Armature

Some people prefer the use of hand and foot armatures. These can help you pose the hand or foot while keeping the finer areas from snapping off accidentally. This is especially useful for hands whose fingers are very thin compared to the rest of the sculpture. Hand armatures can be a simple bent-wire form or simply wires passed down the length of the fingers from the tips. I prefer a two-part hand armature, as shown in Figure 2-8. Since the fingers on a hand move in a different plane from the thumb, this design frees the thumb movement and helps you move the hand as it would move naturally. The wires are placed in the end of a wooden dowel, as shown in Figure 2-8, so the hand can be posed.

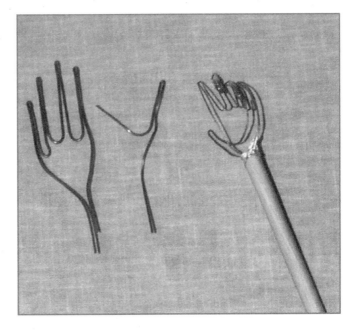

Figure 2-8 *The two-part hand armature, shown left and center, lets you position the hand naturally, as your thumb moves in a different plane from the rest of the hand. On the right, the hand armature wires have been placed in a drilled wooden dowel. The wooden dowel will act as the base for the forearm and can be attached to a wire body armature in the same way it has been attached to the hand.*

If latex masks and prosthetics for aliens with a human-type form are your dream, and you don't want to start your work from scratch, standardized human body forms to be used as armatures are available from Monster Makers.

(See Appendix for more information.) You can then create your creepy-crawly alien skin over the armature. With the parts enhanced with scales, tentacles, or whatever you have in mind, a mold can then be created, allowing you to create the final figure with any number of casting mediums.

Armatures for movable figures, like those used for stop-motion, are more complicated than those that simply hold the figure in a static pose. The complexity of these armatures can range from basic wire forms with ball joints (like the ones I use) to very complex skeletons that resemble the T2000 robot seen in Figures 2-9 a and b.

Figure 2-9 a, b *Some armatures can resemble the complicated T2000 robot, like this one from Sally Corporation. Shown in both standing and sitting positions, the character has all of its valve boards housed beneath it in a stand, because of its complicated movements. The stand is designed to be dropped into the floor, with a finished floor attached for proper appearance.*

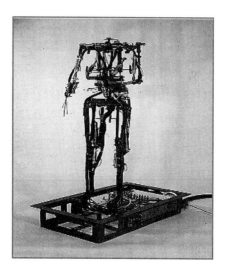 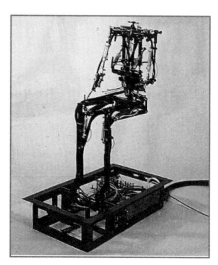

Complex, robotic figures have cables and wires, servos, and remote controls to move the armature from a distance.

High-precision machine shops are needed for building complicated skeletons, to manufacture custom parts so that the skeleton has the appropriate movement at the right scale. There are companies that produce custom armatures. They are typically costly, but for a professional result, it's often worth the extra money. Whichever method you choose for your armature, keep these tips in mind:

- For *static* full-figure sculptures and armatures with ball joints for initial positioning, coat the ball joints with epoxy glue or plumber's putty after positioning the figure, to keep the joints from loosening and moving out of position and to protect them from the disintegrating effects of the clay.

- Polymer clay is expensive and heavy. To avoid creating a full-wire figure including rib cage and so on, and adding unnecessary masses of clay to a maquette figure, use tightly crumpled aluminum foil over the wire armature to build up the interior base before adding a layer of clay. It's much lighter and cheaper.

  Tip: When using foil to build the head interior, keep the aluminum foil from shifting inside the clay by using low-temp hot glue to hold the foil in place. As a by-product, the foil and glue combination also stiffens the armature, The remelting of the glue during clay baking helps to cure the clay on the inside and fills in any air pockets left inside the foil. See Chapter 4 for details on this process.

- If you are using an older digitizing system that picks up the masses of foil, try using Paperclay or plumber's putty as the core. (See Chapter 1 for a discussion of Paperclay.) You must seal Paperclay with something like spray matte finish before applying the polymer clays over it. Otherwise, the polymer won't adhere. For head interiors, lightweight wooden balls also work well.

- If you are using air-dry clay, you can use Styrofoam as an interior for your figure or head. However, never use Styrofoam with clay that is to be baked or fired. The Styrofoam will explode with the heat and release toxic gases.

TIP

ANIMATRONICS

For some, character creation will ultimately result in an animatronic figure animated by cables and wires rather than by computer magic. Like stop-motion figures, animatronic figures must be planned from the armature out, with every detail covered, before the last body covering is applied. Sally Corporation in Florida are experts in the creation of such creatures. They create everything from life-size historical figures, as shown in Figure 2-10, to great fantasy beasts.

Figure 2-10 *Charles Darwin evolved in a matter of weeks from a barebones steel skeleton to a moving, talking animatronic reproduction of the great naturalist. The character, created by the Sally Corporation, welcomes and educates visitors to the St. Louis Zoo's Living World. Photo by Robert Pettus.*

Figure 2-11 *A semifinished cartoon animal character. The Vacu-form head shape is in place on the back of the head, which is also half furred. You can clearly see the cylinders that create the mouth and eye movements. Cylinders coming up from the body into the neck operate the head motions.*

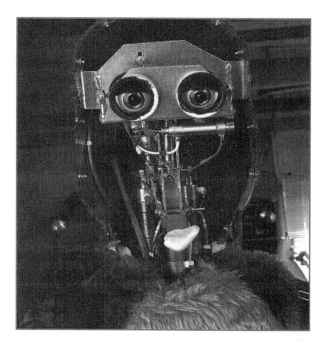

- For movable full-figure sculptures for stop-motion or animatronics, cover each joint with an unlubricated latex condom to keep clay out of the joints. An alternative is to use the cut-off fingers of a surgical glove, although these tend to be more fragile. In either case, you must be sure to attach the sleeve to the armature; otherwise, the clay adheres to the latex and has no contact with the armature.

Their work can be seen at museums, zoos, and amusement parks around the world, including Zombie Paradise: Geopolis in Tokyo, Japan; Granada Television Tour in England; and Disney's wicked Jafar turned cobra in the World on Ice production of *Aladdin*. The technical end of their creations includes steel bodies and pneumatic cylinders, valve boards, and power and air lines to make them move naturally. The head armature seen in Figure 2-11 is an amazing piece of technology that allows the facial expressions and movements to be manipulated in much the same way as the body armatures.

These animated wonders that recreate their roles for viewers day after day are preprogrammed with prepared audiotapes processed into either a CD, a video disc, or tape, depending on the number and complexity of the characters, and then operated in the field through an Animation Control System.

Armatures for Digitizing

As mentioned earlier in this chapter, clay sculptures are being used extensively for digitizing or translating characters from clay into the computer as three-dimensional models. If you will be sculpting life-size or even $^3/_4$-scale head sculptures or larger body sculptures for digitizing, you must use a larger armature—much larger. For digitizing, the piece must be absolutely solid and immovable, so that the digitized positions are accurate and you don't waste time or effort. Nothing exotic is required; the head and armature requirements are described next.

Head Armature for Digitizing

You will need:

- $^3/_8$-inch or $^1/_2$-inch threaded rod from the hardware store.
- A lightweight material applied as the core to take up space and ensure a good connection between the clay and the rod.
- Nuts and washers to fit the threaded rod.
- A flat platform surface.

See Figure 2-12 for an example of this type of stand. Once you create a good digitizing base, it can be reused again and again.

Figure 2-12 *The large digitizing armature is made with $^1/_2$-inch threaded rod secured to $^3/_4$-inch plywood with nuts and washers. The additional nuts and washers at the top will ensure that your rod won't pop through the interior foil and the top of your clay head as you work. This sturdy stand will keep the head from making any unwanted moves during digitizing.*

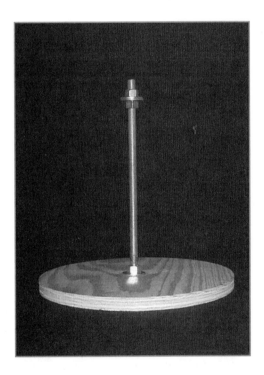

Body Armature for Digitizing

Armatures for digitizing bodies are similar to head armatures in that they are created with large, sturdy rods or even plumbing pipe so that the sculpture is absolutely motionless. The rod can protrude from the body, as shown in Figure 2-13, so that it can hold the sculpture in place even if the body is not perfectly balanced.

The armature is secured to a wooden base, as is the head armature. This type of armature works well with digitizing arms. However, if a laser scanner is to be used to digitize the model, the body may have to be cut apart to get a good reading of the surface, because laser scanners usually aren't as good with "undercuts," or those areas under chins, arms, and other places where it's hard for the laser beam to read.

Figure 2-13 *The sculpture of an alien from the movie* The Arrival *has been created on a strong, sturdy pipe armature to prevent movement of the piece while digitizing.*

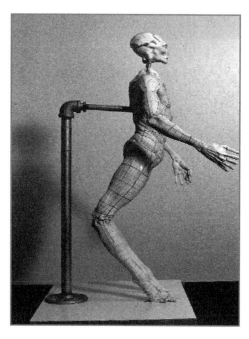

Sculpting Stands

Polymer clays are notorious for becoming soft with the heat of your hands as you work with them. Placing the softened clay in a refrigerator to reharden it works well, but you should avoid manipulating the clay with your hands as much as possible. Some artists prefer to use sculpting stands when working with polymer clays, as shown in Figure 2-14.

The stand needs to be nothing more than threaded rod and a wooden base, but it provides a great way to free your hands and keep the facial features you've worked on so diligently from sliding or being inadvertently pushed off your creation's face. Stands can also come in handy when you are ready for the baking process. (See Chapter 1.)

TIP

KEEPING CLAY WORKABLE

When I'm modeling the clay, I have to confess I just have to hold the clay in my hands. Oh, I've tried to be neat and use a stand. I just can't keep my hands off it. So, to prevent the clay from becoming too soft, I use a trick from master sculptors Richard and Jodi Creager. A pad of clay stuck on the back of the head to rest my fingers on works great. As you will see in Chapter 4, the wooden dowel I use for the interior head armature extends down far enough through the neck to hold on to. This technique lets me hold the head armature while resting my fingers on the pad. When I'm done sculpting, I simply remove the pad from the head.

Figure 2-14 *A small sculpting stand like this one is made for smaller heads, hands, and so on. It helps you sculpt the clay without holding it in your hands, and also acts as an appliance to hold the piece upright as it bakes.*

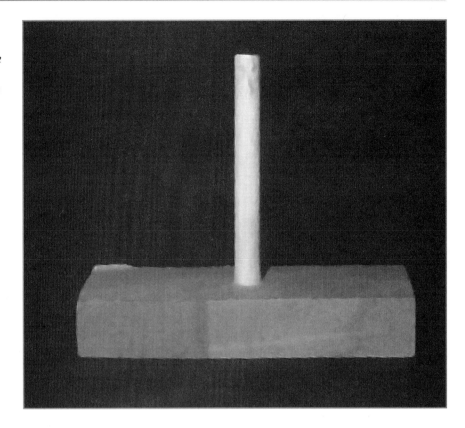

In Conclusion

Whether your figure will be fantasy or reality, it's important to keep in mind that planning is critical for a believable finished product. If you want an old character, sculpt it old completely. Don't just add wrinkles to a young face. If a child is more your speed, make sure that all parts of the face appear the same age. There's nothing quite so disturbing as looking at a so-called child sculpture that has a ten-year-old's nose on a infant-proportioned face.

The armature you build for your character will make or break (a little pun) your sculpture. The best sculpting in the world can't make up for a sagging spine or a maquette that can't hold its own weight. The armature is really the nuts and bolts of sculpting; even though it will be hidden in the final product, it's the most important element for achieving complete success.

In The Next Chapter

In Chapter 3, we'll hear from some of the professionals in the sculpting and model-making field. Read how the aliens were made for the movie *The Arrival* in an interview with Konrad Dunton, head sculptor and senior animator at Pacific Data Images (PDI). Then Mark Siegel and Richard Miller, sculptors at Industrial Light & Magic (ILM), share hints and tips they learned while creating their award-winning creatures. Next, in an interview with Craig Hayes, Art

Director at Tippitt Studios in Berkeley, California, known for stop-motion and sculpting for such great films as *Jurassic Park, Dragonheart,* and *Starship Troopers,* Craig gives us firsthand information about how they create their fabulous creatures. Last, but definitely not least, is an interview with two great master sculptors, Richard and Jodi Creager, known internationally for their fine-art Super Sculpey character figures.

Chapter 3
Interviews with the Masters

Chapter Objectives

Interviews with:

- Konrad Dunton of Pacific Data Images
- Richard Miller and Mark Siegel of Industrial Light & Magic
- Craig Hayes of Tippitt Studios
- Master Sculptors Richard and Jodi Creager

In this chapter we're going to veer off the road somewhat and hear from a select group of working experts in the creative field of sculpting. I think you'll find their hints, tips, and techniques useful for later chapters in this book. While some of our experts are sculptors-in-residence at some of the top animation houses in the entertainment industry, others are world-renowned for their unique, one-of-a-kind character sculptures. I believe both groups have knowledge that you'll find interesting and useful.

The first interview is with Konrad Dunton, head of the modeling department and senior animator with Pacific Data Images (PDI) in Palo Alto, California. Dunton has been with PDI for over 3 years, in which time he's sculpted such memorable characters as the aliens in the movie *The Arrival* and the ice-skating penguins in the Hall's Mentholyptus Lozenges commercial. At the time of the interview, he was working on the Dreamworks 3D animated film *Antz*, with an all-star voice cast including Woody Allen.

In his free time, Dunton teaches courses in computer graphics at California State University at San Jose and also does his own original form of sculpting, as shown in Figure 3-1.

All in all, Dunton is a very talented—and busy—guy.

Figure 3-1 *Konrad Dunton, PDI's master sculptor, with one of his original sculptures.*

Konrad Dunton of PDI

Q: What is your background?

KD: I studied at the University of California at Santa Cruz, with a double major in Computer Graphics and Sculptural Arts, or Fine Arts. Then I worked for Olivetti, creating some computer graphic code for testing a PC graphics accelerator board, so I was writing a graphics library. After that I worked for a Tibetan lama, creating art.

I was just about to leave for New York for a masters degree in Fine Arts at the School of Visual Arts when I got an offer from PDI, and that's how I got in here.

Q: What types of clay do you use for your maquettes and digitizing models at PDI?

KD: We actually don't digitize our own models. We traditionally sculpt with Sculpey, the reason being expediency. It's quickly baked and sent off to the digitizers and it doesn't shrink so you can have an armature inside.

Note: Dunton is referring to the fact that earth clays generally shrink about 20 percent during firing. Any armature be removed and the structure hollowed out before firing, or an explosion can occur.

Q: Do you use Sculpey for your large pieces also?

KD: Yes. Traditionally, the larger pieces are approximately three-quarter human scale, like the alien in *The Arrival*. We had a two-foot character I sculpted [shown in Figure 3-2]. Also, I had a three-quarter head and arm with hand that was sculpted (also in Sculpey) for close-up detail.

Figure 3-2 *The body of the alien for the movie* The Arrival *was sculpted in Sculpey and is approximately 2 feet tall.*

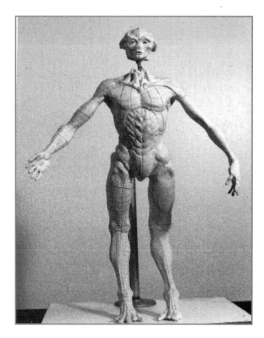

I usually use some sort of interior armature so I don't have to make it solid Sculpey. With a solid Sculpey figure, there's more likelihood of it cracking and falling apart.

Q: What type of armature do you use for your Sculpey figures?

KD: I usually use some kind of plumber's tubing, aluminum armature wire, galvanized steel wire, and aluminum foil for filling up spaces, that kind of stuff. Anything that doesn't fry at 275 degrees goes inside.

Q: Do you have any problems with the aluminum foil and digitizing?

KD: No, none at all. None of the metal inside causes a problem. Originally, many years ago, they were asking us to use wood if possible. So I did work originally with wood dowels. I put everything together with wood, but it was more likely to fall apart in transport. And then they [Viewpoint DataLabs International] got new digitizing equipment that allowed us to use metal again, which was definitely better suited for transportation.

Q: Viewpoint digitizes your models?

KD: Yes. We've worked with them for many, many years and we have a deal for the movie we're working on now; we have two Viewpoint people on site, helping out with the processing of the models. Once the models have been digitized and skinned properly, they come here and we have people who do all kinds of adaptations according to our specific needs.

Q: Does PDI hire sculptors as such or use animators with a knack for sculpting?

KD: We have done both. I tend to sculpt as much as I can to get my hands on the sculpting process. Then, if the pressures are too high and we need more done in a short period of time, we hire from a list we have of sculptors in San Francisco.

Q: How much time do you usually have to produce a maquette or model? Is it always a rush job or does it depend on the project?

KD: It's always a rush job. There's never enough time. I did the Martin Short full-body sculpture [for *A Simple Wish*], and I had about a week or something like that. And that's for the *whole* body, clothes, head, face—everything.

Q: Did you use a body cast for Short?

KD: No, it wasn't full-size. It was just a two-, maybe a little over two-foot high sculpture. So it had to be a miniature. So, no body cast or anything—just some bad pictures that I had to sculpt from.

Q: Do you have facilities on-site to bake the Sculpey or do you have to take it home with you?

KD: Actually, we used to go to the local restaurants to bake our Sculpey. But the sculptures became bigger and bigger, so eventually the ovens didn't work out. At that point, we just built a little wooden box. Well, not that little, you can actually set a human in there! We then put a little oven in the back and have it isolated. It works nice. It's a real good piece of equipment now.

Q: Do you add all the detail possible in the original sculpture or is it added in the computer after the models are digitized?

KD: We try to get everything done in the sculpture. However, the directors can never make up their minds. So it ends up, they approve the sculpture, then in the digitizing process, we tend to lose a little bit of the detail. So we try to fix it up a little bit. That's when the directors come in and they have a whole different idea about what should've been done, and we have to adapt to that. So there's always some detail in the first pass that's added or changed. The second pass occurs most of the time due to the character TDs' [Technical Directors, who set up the characters for motion] requirements. Usually it's an experimental process and we have to go through many iterations before it actually moves properly with the right kind of deformations. So we have to do some modification of shape, some extra added controllers and stuff like that in order to get the shape to bend and look good in motion.

Q: Can you bring the digitized shapes right into your proprietary modeling and animation software or do you use other commercial software?

KD: We go through a lot of filters. There's so much information that has to be added to an Alias or Softimage file format that it takes a few hours of adding all that information. We've streamlined the process, but there are still a lot of filters that get added in order to get from the third-party software to [our] proprietary software.

Q: Are your models laser-scanned or digitized with an arm?

KD: We [have to] go through the process of marking out where our control points and patches are, so a cyberscan-type [laser] approach wouldn't work. It's a manual approach where they go in and touch every little corner … with an arm.

Q: Do you do any body casting, such as with George Clooney's Batman *suit?*

KD: Nope. There's barely any body to be seen anyhow. We actually got that data directly from Viewpoint. We didn't have to be involved in the process of creating the model or the data. We got the data and then had to go through a lot if iterations and processing until finally it was reasonable data. It's the same with any Warner Brothers-type movie. For example, in *Marvin the Martian* they (Warner Brothers) did all the characters. They control that stuff pretty tightly.

Q: What steps do you follow to create a sculpture?

KD: Traditionally, when we need models of something like an animal, I'll start with research. I find images, or have other people run out and get books or images for me.

For the Halls penguin commercials we've done, we went out and got pictures and drawings of penguins, and then created the penguin sculptures. Sometimes I only have drawings. For example, the movie *Antz* has several drawings that are artists' renditions and blueprint-type front and side views.

For a rhino I did a while back [an in-house project], I spent a few days at the zoo sculpting and taking pictures. In that instance, I sculpted from the pictures and the real thing.

In *The Arrival*, we had a little maquette an artist did. Then we made some adaptations to that, then sculpted the real thing with the right pose from the fixed maquette and drawings. That's pretty much the traditional route.

Q: Can you use a maquette for digitizing?

KD: No. They're usually posed in one way or another and are most likely too small for digitizing purposes, so you won't get any detail. A digitized human figure has to be around two feet high. At least that's Viewpoint's recommendation. Anything bigger becomes too much work and it would take more time. You could put in more detail, but it would take much longer. So somewhere around two feet tends to be the size you can sculpt and ship quickly, and get it back at a reasonable rate with enough detail to make it work.

Q: Do you see studios using more digitized clay sculptures? Or will more direct computer-sculpted models be used in the future?

KD: More computer models? I hope not. There's something very relaxing about getting away from the computer and working in clay. And unless you get into sort of a virtual reality modeling, there's no substitute for the three-dimensional experience of a shape. In the computer you are always tied to a two-dimensional view of a three-dimensional object and you always have to move your view around to get a sense of it. But you never really have a true sense of depth and the tools are not as immediate as you would sometimes want to get the organic subtitles that are required for a realistic-looking living thing.

For industrial modeling, it's no big deal at all—the computer is the only way to go. But for living, breathing organic shapes, it's very hard to make the machine do [what you want]. Well, maybe it's not *that* hard, but I don't think it's worth the effort right now, given the software environment, to go that route unless the shapes are rather simple. If they tend to be more complicated, a lot of extremities, stuff like that, it tends to become difficult on the computer; with sculpting, it's just a matter of sticking it on there.

Q: If you're working on a project that has several models that must be similar sizes, how do you standardize the scale?

KD: We tend not to worry about size too much when we're sculpting. Whatever works best for the sculpting process, we do, because once it's in the computer, size is not an issue at all. All you have to do is multiply it by a number and you have a different size.

You usually have to adapt the size anyhow, possibly even from shot to shot and especially when they start animating and say, "Oh man, this one would look much better just a slight bit smaller." And so they change the relationships between characters continuously. It's not like the real world where you have to have those sizes right from scratch, otherwise you have to resculpt the whole thing. There's a big advantage in having a computer in those regards.

Q: What else do you do at PDI?

KD: The things I have been involved with are mainly sculpting, modeling, dealing with the initial [computer] setup, and creating the relationship between mapping and models. I tweak each model, making it good for character setup, and I've done some of my own character setup.

I've also done effects, particle systems, simple drops, and moving things, but the characters themselves get animated by people who specialize in character animation, so I don't do that. Lighting I don't tend to do much either. So, usually everything except character animation and lighting I try to get my fingers into. Although now with the movies, we've been a little more pressed to just focus in one area, which right now is basically modeling and model prep for lighting and character setup.

Q: Do you have any tips you want to share?

KD: Yes. When I was at The School of the Academy of Art in San Francisco, I took a class in Wildlife Sculpture. The best thing that I learned in that class was the approach of using plumbing pipes—elbow joints, tee joints and flanges, stuff like that—to build the initial armature that holds up the sculpture. It's sort of semiexpensive to get all the parts, but once you have the parts, the setup for a great armature that holds up and transports easily is really quick. You just screw it together tight and you're done. It will withstand earthquakes and everything.

Initially I learned to make armatures using wood dowels—screwing, drilling, and bolting. It always took so much more work and so much more time. This is really fast and efficient and it's a strong approach to building armatures.

Mark Siegel and Richard Miller of ILM

Our next interview is with sculptors Mark Siegel and Richard Miller of ILM. Siegel has been with ILM for nine years, while Miller joined ILM at the time of the making of *Return of the Jedi* in 1988. As you will see, they both brought interesting backgrounds to their jobs as sculptors. Some of the characters they've helped create include some of the best-known creatures in the universe, starting with *Return of the Jedi* and continuing to the recent crop of *Special Edition Star Wars* creatures as shown in Figures 3-3 a and b, and those for the *Star Wars* "prequel" trilogy.

Figure 3-3 a *New characters created for the* Special Edition Star Wars *movie are created to digitize into the computer.*

Figure 3-3 b *The sculptors work from drawings to reproduce the characters in clay.*

Q: What are your backgrounds?

RM: I taught sculpture, drawing, and printmaking at junior colleges and universities around California from 1970 to 1980. Then, from 1980 through 1985, I continued to teach part-time while I worked part-time at ILM. For the last fifteen years, I've worked full-time here at ILM.

MS: I didn't have any training as a sculptor at all, actually. I sort of got into it by accident. I was a theater major. Originally, I was trying to get work as an actor. But in my theater training, I had training in makeup, set design, prop-making—all that stuff. I've always made things since I was a little kid.

My connection getting into this business actually came from being a clown in the Ringling Brothers, Barnum and Bailey Circus in 1972. Our makeup teacher in clown school taught me the very first things I'd ever learned about doing prosthetic makeup, casting of faces and making molds and doing sculptures to make our own rubber clown noses, and I sort of took to that. Eventually he wound up giving me my first job at Universal Studios, doing sculptures of masks, prosthetic makeup, and appliances. That turned into a career. I learned a lot about sculpture and mold-making, along with all the materials.

Q: Do you make your maquettes from Super Sculpey?

MS: Yeah, although there're a couple of different ways we're going, now that we're doing the "scanning thing." We're doing our original design maquettes in Super Sculpey. That's for the art director and George Lucas to finalize the design. But those Sculpey figures usually don't work for scanning because we're sculpting them in active positions, giving them character expressions, and they're also pretty small. So the ones we end up doing for the scanner are the larger size. We're sculpting those in Plastalina and then making molds and plastic castings that they scan. [See Figure 3-4.]

Q: Then you're using a laser scanner rather than an arm?

RM: Yeah. We have our own scanner now. In the past we used to take it to a place that did the scanning, and then the scanning information was put on the computer. We have to cut up the figures in pieces in some cases so they can get a good reading.

Q: Don't laser scanners have problems with undercuts?

RM: That's exactly part of the problem at the moment. They're working on software that will overcome that, and for all I know, next week they'll figure that out. But at the moment, we're cutting arms off and separating the legs from the body to scan them.

MS: I had slightly different information than Richard did. As far as I understand it, for sculptures that I've been doing recently (say it's a four-legged animal), they want us to keep the sculpture to a size that allows it to fit into the scanning bed, for instance, no more than about twelve inches tall. I think they've been taking them whole and just putting them in the scanner and the laser is able to rotate around the creatures to enable it to read all the undercuts. I think the last few they haven't had to take apart.

Figure 3-4 *Facial features are being sculpted for digitizing in plastilina.*

RM: Well, no, see Mark and I work in the same department, but we don't necessarily talk, and I noticed when I looked at the last figure you did, Mark, (the last four-legged creature), they were bringing it back over to the shop to saw its legs off. They tried, but it just wasn't working as well as it did with sawing them off.

MS: It probably also has something to do with each individual case. With the last sculpture I did, I know the legs were very close together and it might have been more difficult for the scanner to read in-between things; and maybe in another case if there's more space between the legs, or somehow underneath, maybe it works better. So it's probably a very individual process.

Q: How much detail do you include on your digitizing models? It seems that with a scanner you would be able to use quite a bit of detail and get it into the computer model.

RM: That goes two ways. We hear on one hand that you don't need much detail, you just need the general structure and muscle structure and stuff of that nature. And that the surface painter, the person who will be putting on the surface texture and a variety of other details, is the person who will really do the fine detail. However, we do the fine detail in the sculpture because the artist and the art director and everybody else has to see what it looks like, including the person who will paint it in the computer. So finishing the detail is very important; it's just that at this point, the scanner doesn't pick up that fine detail.

MS: I, again, have a little different take on it. In general, what Richard says is right, we do finish sculptures with scales and wrinkles and whatever skin texture there is, because then the finished model is a good reference model for the computer artists; they paint it and they use it while they're building the model. However, the CG guys say that all the detail we're putting on actually gets in the way in the scanning process. The latest generation scanner is picking up lots of detail, and it's picking up more detail than they want, in fact it's giving them too much information. So when they go back to refine it for their computer model, they have to get rid of some of that extra stuff that the scanner has picked up. So, in one way, they would really like it if we gave them a really nice shape with a defined musculature, that would give them a nice clean scanning model. But, on the other hand, they like the finished skin detail model because that gives them a final reference. I know there are different systems for doing the skin texture. The one I believe we use at ILM, all that skin texture, fine wrinkles, scales, bumps, and whatever, is done by painting the CG model using 3D painting software.

Q: What kind of armatures do you use for your maquettes?

RM: We're using aluminum armature wire because the size doesn't demand anything more than that, and we even fill some of the larger volumes up with aluminum foil if there's going to be a lot of volume here and there. Sometimes we'll carve some rigid foam. We've found that some of the urethane foam we carve from is good for substructure. It's light and coats well with the Sculpey and Plastalina.

TIP

ARMATURE HELP

One material we love to use with the armatures is Plumber's Putty. It's a two-part material with the consistency of a thick dough that usually comes in a tube like a big Tootsie Roll. The inner core is one component of the epoxy and the outer core is the other component. When you cut a piece off and knead it together, the epoxy parts blend and then, within about 10 to 15 minutes, it dries rock-hard. We can use that for molding together some of the armature wire, building up some of the areas inside. It's really an extremely handy tool. The kind we use is ProPoxy; it's just a hardware store item.

Q: So, it doesn't explode when you bake the Super Sculpey?

MS: The heat's not high enough in the [Super] Sculpey. You couldn't do that in a lot of other materials, but when we're doing our [Super] Sculpey for the maquettes, we put them in the oven and it only goes up to 200 to 300 degrees. With Plastalina, we don't have to put it in the oven at all. And like Richard said, with the [Super] Sculpey figures, we usually fill out the bulk with aluminum foil. It's in the bigger ones we do in Plastalina that we use foam.

Figure 3-5 *A rhino from the movie* Jumanji *has wrinkles and other small detail applied.*

Q: Are you still using stop-motion figures for any of your shots?

MS: That seems to be pretty rare now, at least at this shop. Stop-motion is pretty much a thing of the past. Any background creatures or full animated things are just being done with CG models now.

RM: Or some practical, simple sculptures.

MS: Oh yeah, we have been doing full-sized puppets for some shots. These are not stop-motion puppets, but hand puppets or partial body or rod-controlled puppets. [See Figure 3-6 a, b, and c.]

Figure 3-6 a *A large version of the snapping tail from* Dragonheart *is created to use as a full-size puppet. (Taken from a video screeen.)*

Figure 3-6 b *Another sculpture is created for the dragon's mouth in* Dragonheart.

Figure 3-6 c *A partial body sculpture can be used as a rod puppet.*

Q: What materials do you use on your rod-type puppets?

MS/RM: That varies depending on what it is and what it has to do and how big it is. The standard for really fine facial movements and a real soft skin is foam latex. But we can often get away with using a painted latex skin that's painted into the mold and filled with a soft urethane foam for bigger body parts. For example, did you see the *Special Edition Return of the Jedi?* We built a new puppet for the musicians in Jabba's palace. It's the fat green guy who plays the space harmonica. That had a combination of things. The head was foam latex, and that was foamed up and baked as foam latex has to be, and the core of the mold was shaped to fit my hand,

Figure 3-7 *A maquette from the movie* Casper *appears in the background as an ape head from the movie* Jumanji *is being fine-tuned.*

so as I put my hand and my fingers into that face, I could move the foam latex and get lots of little subtle expressions and movements.

The body, arms, and the other hand, that didn't have to have fine movement, were just done with latex skin filled with soft urethane foam. They had hard-jointed, aluminum armatures inside of those arms and legs anyway, and inside the body was just a big foam shell. So we used a combination of materials. The advantage of latex skin and foam fill is that it's a lot faster than foam latex and easier to deal with in large molds, because it doesn't have to be baked. That creature was sculpted in Plastalina over an armature and then plaster molds were made. Then the process we just explained was done.

MS: There are even times we won't sculpt and do molds. We'll sculpt direct if it's appropriate, by taking sheets or blocks of soft foam, like mattress foam, and carve and shape it to the various body parts. Then we'll skin it with some type of latex or other skin material, or even fur. I think that was the case with the Wampa suit, which wasn't really a puppet, it was sort of a combination puppet and suit for *Empire Strikes Back.*

Q: Do you use a specific type of paint on the latex?

RM: A lot of painters end up having different specifics, but I remember rubber-cement-based paint.

MS: Rubber-cement-based paint is really the best because it's flexible and it really sticks to the latex or the foam. It's essentially taking store-bought rubber cement and thinning it down with the appropriate solvent and adding pigment to it. You're actually painting rubber cement on the foam rubber part, so it sticks really well, it's completely flexible. You have to powder it after you spray or paint it on because it still remains tacky, but once it's powdered it becomes a great coating.

For smaller details, there's a paint they call PAX which is really a mixture of acrylic paint and medical adhesive and that's mixed up in small quantities and used to paint on generally finer detail stuff, like faces and things like that. It's also very strong and flexible.

Q: What do you use for fur on your finished puppets?

MS: We frequently have to add fur on puppets or suits. We get fur from a number of places. Generally it's from a place called Hair Technologies, Inc. in New York. They have a wide variety that we can even custom order. We can tell them exactly the color we want or we can give them a swatch, and we can get blends of different fur, synthetic or natural hair, just about anything we want. Some come on a four-way stretch backing.

Occasionally we will actually embed the hair into a foam backing. We take some of the same foam latex that we use for molds and spread it out with a spatula into a thin sheet and then press the hair into it. We then trim the back off the foam, so what we've done is replace the knit backing that the hair comes on with this sheet of foam that has hair embedded into it. Then that becomes a real flexible backing we can glue onto finished puppets.

Q: What background does someone need to become a sculptor?

RM: Sculpture, as it used to be, is going out. All they really need at this point—for computers specifically—is sculptors to do maquettes or models that they scan.

Now, I know from my friends in the CG department that they are going in that direction more and more and using scanned objects. So that bit of work is still available. However, there are still some large or other approaches to puppets and sculpture that include the old-fashioned sculpting techniques. With that little disclaimer, you can still take sculpting classes at any junior college or art school. You can do it on your own, read magazines, look at books on sculpting—anything of that nature to keep your hand in doing naturalistic sculpture.

MS: The best way to sculpt well is just do a lot of it. The more you do, the more you just naturally become adept with the material and start figuring out techniques. [You also need to study,] not necessarily anatomy, but some sort of sculpture classes that give you a chance to sculpt from nature, from a model or from photographs of animals. This is really valuable because of all the work we do for film. Almost all the work we do for film *is* creating creatures of some sort. So it is important to be familiar with musculature.

Abstract sculpture, although personally I love it, has very little application here. Many of the art schools where they offer sculpture classes tend toward commercial gallery art. If you want to be in this business, you would probably be wasting a lot of time by going that route.

Q: What are the favorite creatures you've worked on at ILM?

MS: A little disclaimer here: I don't create characters here. A couple of my favorite things I have worked on have been *Ghostbusters,* the original movie. I worked on the Slimer character. Although, like I said, I didn't really create it, I was just part of the team. I did some of the sculpture and some of the fabrication, but he was really a fun character to work on from my standpoint, since I came from a performing background as an actor. One of the things that really makes me enjoy working on a character is being able to follow it through as a puppeteer and start bringing it to life. I believe that's why I liked the Slimer character so much. I was not only getting to work on the sculpting of it, but I got to be part of the performing team as well. When the character came to life, he really was as funny in real life as he was on the screen, maybe even funnier. We just really had a good time operating that character.

I had a similar fun experience doing a Godzilla suit. Richard also worked on that one here for a Nike commercial where Charles Barkley played basketball with Godzilla. That was also really fun. In general, I've been having a great time doing the new *Star Wars* characters. There's just a spirit about it that makes it a lot of fun for me. Richard and I each have done dozens of new character sculptures, and so without being specific (as we can't even tell you what we're doing), that has been a favorite for me.

RM: I started out in *Return of the Jedi* and did Princess Leia's metal bikini. The reason that I feel good about that, is that I had more input in that than anything else afterward. I was chosen by Milos Roda, who was the art director, because of the sculpture I did. During that period of time I was still teaching and doing my own sculpture. So I got to do a little bit of the designing on that. As Mark said, we often don't get to design anything. We may add a little bit to it, but it's not really our original designs, so that was my favorite.

The only other area I feel comfortable mentioning is when we do a naturalistic animal or whatever. I did the whales for *Star Trek IV,* which a lot of people didn't even know were puppets. Again, all I was doing was copying nature, so I really didn't have an art director to deal with. So those are the things I like to do. I did a number of the creatures in *Jumanji* and a few other things of that nature, naturalistic animals or people puppets in cockpits and pilots and stuff like that. I think Princess Leia's outfit and the whales in *Star Trek IV* were the most successful.

Q: Who has control over a character's design?

MS: Ultimately it's the Director of the film; he has the final say. And then down from there, there's an art director usually on every film, and that art director with their team, whoever it is, would come up with drawings of the characters, that again have to be approved by the director. So every film has a different art director.

Doug Chang is the guy who's art directing the new *Star Wars* and he has very specific ideas about how he wants the characters to look. He has a team that generates drawings and once they're approved by George, he brings them down to Richard and me and we sculpt the maquettes. But then Doug is there every day and gives his comments about what shapes he wants us to work on or refine or whatever in the sculptures. So, really the art director is probably the most directly responsible, and then ultimately has to answer to the director's vision.

Craig Hayes of Tippitt Studios

Next we hear from Craig Hayes, Art Director of Tippitt Studios in Berkeley, California. Tippett Studios was founded by Phil Tippett, and has been one of the most successful "creature shops" since its inception. Hayes has worked at Tippitt Studios for 11 years. He no longer sculpts himself, but he is in charge of the creature design process and the sculptors who build them. Hayes originally came from a model-building background in industrial design and has created props for rock videos.

Q: Do you have more control over the actual design than the sculpting itself?

CH: Yes. I usually start out with a 2D drawing. I do the drawings and then work with the sculptor to get the maquettes sculpted out.

Q: How is clay sculpting used at Tippitt Studios these days, since stop-motion, where Tippett made its mark, isn't used as much anymore?

CH: Right. We're doing more computer graphics using maquettes and digitizing models to create computer models.

Q: Are you using any of the stop-motion figures at all?

CH: We use a variation of them. We build these stop-motion-type armatures with sensors on them so we can register their movement. So, we do a lot of animation with input devices like the DID [Dinosaur Input Device].

Q: In what scale do you usually sculpt your maquettes?

CH: It runs the range, but generally in the area of one-tenth scale. It depends on how big the character is. If it's forty feet long, then obviously we'll work at something like one-twentieth scale. But usually one-tenth is a pretty good estimation.

Q: What types of clay are you using?

CH: Most the time we use Super Sculpey.

Q: Do you have anything on-site you use to bake your characters?

CH: Yes, we have an oven to bake the figures in.

Q: And it's big enough for all your figures?

CH: Yes. We did a lot of stuff back when we were doing lots of foam latex, so we got a large oven. Also, you can use a hair dryer or a heat gun to harden the clay.

Q: Do you have any tips on working with the clays?

CH: Basically, really plan everything out. We start from a 2D source, a drawing or design, and then go into three dimensions. [See Figures 3-8a, b, and c.]

Q: What size wire do you use for your armatures?

Figure 3-8 a *A sculpture of Draco the dragon for the movie* Dragonheart *is being created from drawings and schematics.*

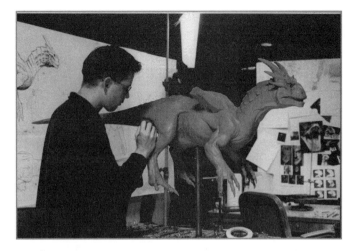

Figure 3-8 b *Phil Tippett and Pete Konig with two of the Draco maquettes. Making the armature is probably the most critical part. Make a good, strong wire armature that's got a lot of detail on it so the clay really sticks.*

Figure 3-8 c *Finished maquette of Draco with Bowen.*

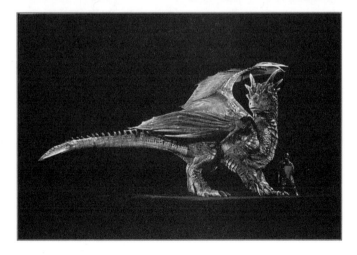

CH: We use $1/8$-inch to $3/16$-inch wire, and like that, smaller for fingers. We also use hand and feet armatures for our figures, so basically, the whole figure has an armature base.

Q: What types of sculpting tools do you use?

CH: I use basic sculpting tools, the wire tools and so on. Everyone has their own favorites, but I use just the basic sculpting tools.

Q: Do you have any problems with clay breaking or cracking?

CH: If you're going to build a big mass of clay, you're always going to have problems like that. Usually, it's a good idea to use aluminum foil to flesh out on top of the armature and bulk it up so the clay can be kept relatively thin, instead of having a big solid chunk. When we do this, we don't have too much trouble with breaking. Also, generally we sculpt our parts with removable arms and such, especially when we know a part will be particularly hard to get to for the scanner.

Q: Do you digitize in-house?

CH: Yes, we do.

Q: Do you use laser scanners or digitizing arms?

CH: We built our own digitizing arm. We made it a while ago when we couldn't afford one, so we just made it.

Q: Do you use proprietary software?

CH: No. Well, for digitizing we do, but no modeling software. We bring it into Softimage and generally refine the model there. The digitizing software produces a model that can go directly into Softimage.

Q: How much time do you usually have to produce a project?

CH: Oh, it's pretty varied. It depends on the complexity of the model, and how it's going to be used. Is it close-up or far away, how many pieces, and what kind of paint job do we have to do? For *Starship Troopers*, for instance, it would probably be quantified in months.

Q: What kinds of paints do you use on your models?

CH: Mostly we're using Tamiya paints. We use a lot of airbrush, drybrush, and like that.

Q: What have been your favorite projects to work on in the 11 years you've been with Tippitt?

CH: Robocop. I liked that one. *Honey, I Shrunk the Kids* I thought was an excellent film. But *Starship Troopers* is the peak in some ways. [See Figures 3-9 a and b.]

Q: I hear Starship Troopers *is gory.*

CH: Yeah, but it's kind of a good gore. It's like a Dutch painting versus *Rambo*. Paul Verhoeven's got a different take on violence.

Q: What background do you consider important for people who are interested in working as sculptors for Tippitt Studios?

CH: Sculpture, painting, life drawing, photography are good mechanical skills. Musical backgrounds are helpful to give a little diversity, and then a general regular athletic program.

Q: Do you use your animators as sculptors, or do you hire sculptors individually?

CH: Well, we still group it as we have done in the past. We have an art department that has many people with different skills. So, we tend to rely on them for sculpting. Also, a couple of the sculptors are animators. So, yes some animators do sculpt but it's not that we tell our animators,

Figure 3-9 a *Sculptors work on the hopperbug maquettes from the movie* Starship Troopers.

Figure 3-9 b *Wings for insects in* Starship Troopers *are being created and will be applied to the finished maquette.*

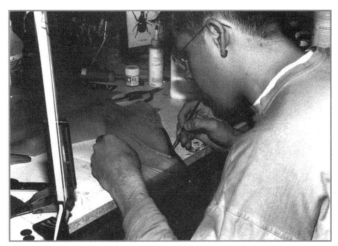

"Now you're going to sculpt." It's more that people who have been sculpting become animators.

Q: Do you use Plastalina for your larger models?

CH: No, generally we use Super Sculpey for everything; it works pretty well. Or we use Das; it's a more powdery compound that works pretty well too.

Q: Do you make molds from your originals?

CH: Yes. We actually don't work off the original Super Sculpey figures. We make molds off all of them. We use a silicon molding compound and plaster to make molds. Then we digitize off our molded copies. That's important because we usually create several maquettes. One is a fully painted maquette; one is an unpainted maquette so we can draw the lines on it and so on.

Q: Do you try to put as much detail as you can into the models you're going to digitize, or do you add it later in the computer?

CH: The detail is definitely in the model before we digitize it. But [as for] the digitizing that we do, we digitize to a lower degree of detail, and then we paint the detail back in with the computer.

Q: Do you use the painted maquettes as models for the computer artist to paint the CG character?

CH: The animators don't paint them; the art department paints them. We use the painted maquettes as reference and then we paint them, get them all set up, and then create a low resolution version for the animators to animate with.

Richard and Jodi Creager of Creager Doll Studios

When I first started sculpting with Super Sculpey seven or eight years ago, there was very little information available on the subject, save trial and error (many trials and a whole lot of errors). I was fortunate, though, enough to meet a very talented couple who shared their techniques and knowledge about sculpting with this medium and saved me hundreds of hours of manic headbanging.

Our final interview is with this very talented couple, Richard and Jodi Creager. They have been sculpting and selling original character figures for some 15 years. They have sold their figures internationally, and countless collectors, including celebrities such as Demi Moore and Richard Simmons, find their work as expressive and imaginative as you will. Although the figures are sometimes called dolls by the general public, this term is really a misnomer; they are one-of-a-kind or limited series artworks that are created for display, not play.

Because they work as a team, their approach to figure-making is a little different from others you have read about in this chapter. The Creagers' figures are sometimes made with cloth bodies, clothed and outfitted with extravagant accessories. At other times, beautiful clay bodies are sculpted. Everything you see on and with these figures is custom made and one-of-a-kind. There are no molds involved in their work, even in their limited series. Even the shoes are made meticulously by hand.

In the Creager team, each has his or her own areas of expertise. Jodi sculpts heads and hands and paints each piece with expert care. She also makes the intricate clothing, custom wigs the heads by hand, and applies even the smallest detail—each individual fingernail is applied separately, one at a time. Richard, a true perfectionist and craftsman in metal and clay, has his own specialties. He sculpts legs and bodies. He also painstakingly builds the wire armatures and every type of accessory used in their unique art. Together they create amazing figures. Although Richard doesn't sculpt the wonderful expressive faces—that's Jodi's area—he is accomplished himself when it comes to sculpting. The magnificent mother dog sculpted for one of their tableaus, shown in Figure 3-10 is his work.

Even though their Super Sculpey figures are the end product of their fine-art sculptures, rather than an intermediate step as with digitized models, the Creagers' knowledge is priceless for anyone wishing to know more about using this medium.

Note: The Creagers have recently produced the first videotape in a series teaching their sculpting techniques. You can learn more about it in the Appendix.

Figure 3-10 *The mother watches carefully as the dalmation puppies are carefully "spotted" by their owner.*

Q: What is your background and how did you start making dolls and character figures?

RC: Actually, Jodi started in 1977 when we moved to Oregon. She started needle-sculpting [a technique for creating soft sculpture using a needle and thread on a cloth figure] and we started out with craft items. We were also doing cloth dolls made to order for people that were a little more complex. I helped with accessories. Jodi at that point turned it into a business. I hurt my back and came into the business with her full-time.

JC: We continued to do shows and then moved down to California. We didn't know what a doll show was, but someone told us ours could actually cross over into the doll world. So we went to a doll show and were blown away.

In 1989, we started working with Super Sculpey when we were commissioned along with eleven other California artists by the Sacramento History Museum to do figures pertaining to history, folklore, and legends of the West. The artists came from all parts of the state, and since we were in the Sierra foothills, we decided to do the gold hardrock miners and tommy-knockers (little elfins that protect miners in the cave). I could have done the larger miners in soft sculpture, but couldn't figure out a way to do the tiny tommy-knockers, and that's when I discovered Super Sculpey. That's what opened the door. Everyone reacted to those, and we never did another soft sculpture again.

Richard and I were elected to N.I.A.D.A. [National Institute for American Doll Artists] in 1991. Our dolls are on display as a fine-art medium in museums and galleries throughout the United States and Europe.

Q: Do you have any formal art education background?

RC: I did. I have some drawing and art education and I graduated from Brooks Institute in Santa Barbara with a degree in photography. Though it was primarily photographic work, it did include classes in composition and the related art fields. Everything else is self-taught.

JC: Art has always been important in our lives … and it was art that brought us together. Richard's artistic prowess lies in the technical and mechanical field; his father, a Union Pacific Railroad engineer, piqued his interest in metal and machines. I come from a family of musicians, actors, scenic artists, writers, and lighting directors, so my interest in the arts was inevitable. I began painting at a very early age; people were my subject. Totally self-taught, I earned my living as a portrait artist. I only had two art lessons in my life. I didn't get along with the teacher, so I never went back.

Q: What type of clay do you use?

JC: Strictly Super Sculpey. We've tried them all, experimented with everything including mixing, which I don't like. We started with Super Sculpey and we stuck with it because it worked well. I think your medium finds you. I've tried other ones and I can't work with them. Super Sculpey is just perfect for us.

Q: What tips do you have regarding working with the clay?

JC: Well, the big question was always how to get fingerprints out, smooth it and get a glass-like surface. I've tried all kinds of things. One of the things I do—and people are always amazed at this when I teach classes—I use the finest emery board, the pink one you use for buffing the top part of your nails, and I buff my fingertips before smoothing the clay.

I also rub a polished, smooth agate stone wetted with saliva on the surface of the clay figure before it's baked. That really works. Or, if you don't want to spit on your creation, you can place it in the freezer and freeze it hard. Then use your agate stone with the moisture that has condensed on the surface of the clay to give it the same smoothed finish.

RC: Also, using a soft brush to smooth areas hard to reach with your fingers is very effective. That removes the tool marks and fingerprints and works well in detailed areas like those around the eyes.

JC: I've also used acetone with a small brush, but I don't like to use that until the final touch. If you use too much it tends to disintegrate the Sculpey and you'll get white residue afterward. You can also try a few drops each of the Sculpey Diluent and mineral spirits [paint thinner] because it won't eat at the clay, but will provide a smooth finish.

Q: What types of armatures do you use?

RC: Well, since there are two of us working as a team, she has her part and I have mine. The armatures on my part of the figure (the legs and body) are all soldered brass rods. I work up a diagram on how we're going to position the figure so it can react to the environment we have planned for it. For example, if one foot is going to be raised on a slope of ground, then we have to plan for that ahead of time because once the armatures are set, they're not re-posable at all. They're pretty sturdy. [See Figure 3-11.]

Also, we create our figures so the foot is pinned onto a peg attached to the base. This way it will be secured to the base, but when you take it off the base it doesn't have a peg coming out of the foot of the figure.

Figure 3-11 *One of Santa's elves takes a turn at the ice. The feet are secured to the base with tubing and wire.*

There's just a hole through the bottom of the foot and up through the leg with a metal tube inside that is soldered onto the internal skeleton. This allows the weight of the figure to be held by the armature and not the clay.

JC: The reason he solders is because the bottom part of the body (which he does) needs the strength, so there won't be any kind of bending in the ankles or any other movement. Some people just use foil and wire, but it has too much movement. This is solid and rigid so it won't crack the clay and it can take a lot of weight.

RC: Since we sell to collectors, you don't want them moving it around and having an ankle snap.

Q: What diameter rod do you use with your 18-inch figures?

RC: I use $^3/_{32}$-inch brass brazing rod. You can get it at a welding supply shop. It's cheaper than buying it at brass supply houses. The leg armature is three rods soldered together. You get a dimensional strength that way. It's harder to bend and makes for a really strong armature. You don't have to worry about the ankles cracking.

Q: Do you use soft solder or silver solder?

RC: Soft solder. I tried silver solder and it doesn't flow quite as well, and I don't think it has the strength. With soft solder, even if you don't get the best joint, it takes quite a bit of effort and a pair of pliers to bend it.

Q: Do you solder the entire length of the wire?

RC: Yes. The entire lengths of the three wires are soldered.

JC: He has two big torches, but he just discovered through a company called Micromark a great little canister butane torch that is as hot as the other ones he has, but easier to handle and use.

RC: It's a 2,000-degree flame and it just runs on butane. It has the little piezoelectric thing in it so it has a self-starter. It has a nice little knife-like flame. Really nice.

Q: Do you use acid or rosin core solder?

RC: I use a rosin core solder, but an acid flux.

Q: If you are sculpting whole body torsos, how do you keep the clay from cracking?

RC: We do figures that are entirely sculpted in clay, and figures with cloth bodies that have sculpted arms, legs, shoulders, and heads. On an armature I'm using a sculpted clay body on, I've found that the clay will crack as it expands and contracts during the cooling period. For that type of armature, I've found that I need to give it collapsibility so that it won't break the clay during contractions. I build the spine in two parts out of $1/4$-inch brass rod. I attach a $1/4$-inch inside diameter brass tube along the lower half of the spine, leaving enough room so it can contract a little bit. Then I silver-solder the tube onto the lower spine. The top part of the spine, which includes the ribcage, is the $1/4$-inch rod which will slip down into the tube attached to the lower section. I lay out my skeleton on a graph I have drawn depicting the size of my figure so the length will be correct. I position the $1/4$-inch rod into the tube and then adjust so the shoulder girdle and the pelvis are the correct length apart, and I put a little hot[-melt] glue on the joint where the tubing and rod come together. This allows the spine to stay in place as you're sculpting. Then when you cure it in the oven, the hot glue liquefies and allows just enough movement so cooling contractions won't crack the Sculpey.

Q: What about the upper half of the armature?

JC: That would be my part. Hands and heads are my areas.

In heads, I use a $1/4$-inch wooden dowel with a penny attached. This is covered with foil and hot glue. More foil and then Super Sculpey is applied. [Details of this technique are described in Chapter 4.]

For the hands, I use 20-gauge floral wire and $1/4$-inch wooden dowel. A hole is drilled through the center of the dowel about $3/4$-inch deep. I shape my hand out of the wire. The wooden dowel allows you to bend the hand at the wrist and gives you a good base to attach the arm to the body armature. When I have it bent to the shape I want it, I pose it in the position the hand will be in and cover it with foil, which I adhere with hot glue. When the hand is exactly like I want it, I build my clay on that. It lasts longer, doesn't break as easily, and it's good for position and strength when the figure is holding something.

RC: One of the big advantages to using an armature like that is you can work out the pose for the hand if it's going to be holding a particular item and have it posed perfectly ahead of time; then you're just adding the flesh to it and detail. You don't have to try and manipulate the hand after you have the Sculpey on it.

Q: What techniques do you use for the arms and shoulders?

JC: If the arms will be bare, I'll create a breastplate that will come down to meet the top of the arms. I use the same principle here as I did with the hand. I use the $1/4$-inch dowel coming out of the hand to go into the interior of the mid-lower arm. A second dowel is used for the upper arm and wire is wrapped around the lower and then the upper dowels to hold them together. Foil is then wrapped over the dowel and hot[-melt] glue is spread all around to hold foil on. The arm is bent into position and then Super Sculpey is applied, leaving some of the top wooden dowel exposed. Now the arm can be baked.

Right when the arm comes out of the oven, still hot, just take that dowel that's exposed on the upper arm and give it a twist. The hot glue is re-liquefied and allows you to pull that dowel out of the arm, leaving a nice hollow. The wire that comes out of the body now goes right down that hollow to attach the arms onto the body.

RC: It works out better to have some flexibility in the upper part of the armature, unlike the rigid legs, so you can fine-tune the pose if the figure will be holding something.

JC: If you're sculpting something like a maquette, you can use the same technique. Just sculpt the torso, bake it, add the arm, bake it, and then add the shoulder area last to create the final pose, and bake it again to complete the body.

Q: Since your sculptures are final products rather than an intermediate step to a digitized piece, what types of paint do you use on your figures?

JC: All water-based stuff. I have tried oils, but I don't have the patience. If I'm doing African American skin tones, I use anywhere from 25 to 35 coats of thin washes of paint and I apply them all in layers and shade. But always acrylic paints. Also chalk pastels for coloration like the cheeks, highlights, stuff like that. [See Figure 3-12.]

Figure 3-12 *The beautiful black angel with baby has been painted with many layers of washes to achieve the right skin tones.*

Q: What do you do to preserve it?

JC: I like Krylon Matte Finish Spray number 1311. You have to watch for that specific number because they have a new one that has come out which is the low-odor, environmentally safe one. It's very bad for our purposes. It spews white flecks out onto your figure, and it's shiny and terrible! Also, you might note that if you want to maintain a matte finish on your figure, you have to hold the spray can out at an arm's distance from the clay surface, and spray very lightly. Two or three coats are advisable.

For the last coat, spray a mist in the air and then run the figure through it to give a very light last coat. If you hold it too close or for too long, you'll end up with a shiny, plastic-looking finish, which defeats all the work you've put into the figure to make it look natural.

Q: Polyform Products is introducing a new product, Premo, to add to Super Sculpey to give it a little more flexibility. Do you think that's going to affect the paint?

JC: I don't think it's going to make any difference. I haven't used it yet, but I don't think it will affect the paint. When I paint now, I use many thin washes. The paint beads up on the [oil-based] clay surface, because water and oil will have that reaction. I put it on very quickly and then I blot it and smooth it with a cloth. Once you have the first two coats on, you don't have to worry about it beading up; at that point there's enough paint covering the surface to accept the paint.

Q: What type of sculpting tools do you use?

JC: I use dental tools, the spoon type. Richard makes all my fingernail tools and toenail tools. Palette knives are great for removing thin little pieces of clay instead of pinching them off. It will actually work better than an X-acto knife to shave the Sculpey off without pulling the Sculpey and dragging pieces with it. It cuts real nice. But I like the dental tools for sculpting; they're my favorite. I also use reference models as I work, like ears, skulls, et cetera. [See Figure 3-13.]

Figure 3-13 *Reference models are available to use while sculpting. Here are a few that Jodi uses as she sculpts.*

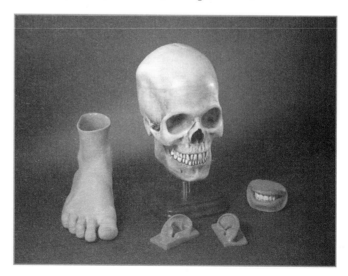

Q: How does Super Sculpey hold up over time?

JC: That's an interesting question. I have seen artists' dolls from the 1960s made out of Super Sculpey. The girl who originally sculpted Yoda, Wendy Froud, says she has used it for many years and it's kept fine. (She and her husband, Brian Froud, who wrote *The Fairy Book*, worked on both *The Dark Crystal* and *Labyrinth*. In fact, their son was the baby in *Labyrinth*.)

E.J. Taylor, a wonderful English sculptor and artist, uses Super Sculpey that he's had since the beginning of his career in the 1980s. He treats it like fine wine he's aging. The earlier Super Sculpey was harder, with a longer shelf life. [Polyform Products changed the formula to meet government requirements for nontoxicity, so] the stuff they're making now has less of the nasty stuff, but has a shorter shelf life and, long-range, it's hard to tell how it's going to keep. But I have total faith in it. However, like any other medium you should follow some basic precautions:

- Keep stored figures away from fluorescent lights. You wouldn't store fine paintings that way.
- Don't overuse or overhandle it. The oils from your hands also have adverse affects on the clay. I think if you give it respect, it's going to last as long as you allow it to last.

I have never heard of anything just completely crumbling, and every time I *have* heard of something falling apart, it's because the clay has been mixed, or the artist mishandled it. They overbaked it, underbaked it, or worked air into it. Years ago, it was a big thing to mix oil paints into the Super Sculpey for color, before they knew they could just paint the surface. A lot of people did early blacks that way. They would glob the paints in and knead the paints and clay together, then sculpt. This sort of mixing is sure to have a reaction. So I always stress using pure Super Sculpey. Pro-Mat or the new Premo is all right to mix with Super Sculpey, because it's made to be chemically compatible.

I hear a lot of talk at shows about Cernit. People mix it with Super Sculpey and I hear, "Cernit is so great because it has that wonderful translucent look." I tell them, "Our faces aren't translucent; what are you talking about, natural look?" Do they think we look like jellyfish?

Q: In what scale do you work?

JC: The largest head I usually do is approximately three inches tall. However, I can use my sculpting techniques to sculpt any size head. I'd just adjust the sizes of my armatures and appliances.

RC: I think on a much larger head, you have to work up some sort of armature inside that has flexibility, like that of the body. The more Super Sculpey you have, the more the clay will contract as it's cooling, so you have to have something inside that has some give to it.

JC: I have heard people who use wooden egg shapes for the interior of the head.

RC: Yes, but I've also heard that they have a lot of cracking.

JC: Sometimes the baking can bring moisture out of the wood even though the wood appears to be dry. That's why I feel totally confident in using the foil and hot glue inside my heads; it allows the clay to expand and then when it cools down, it allows the melted hot glue which is trapped in there to recongeal and also fill in any air bubbles. I have not had one head crack since I've been using this method. I used to have cracks through the temples and the bridge of the nose horizontally, as the longest length of the head contracted.

RC: In the body, we encountered the same problem, with the length of the torso pushing and pulling and so cracking around the center horizontally. So that's where you have to allow for movement. Another thing to note on the leg armatures is that I have no problem with the legs when they're fairly straight, because the Super Sculpey can contract and slide down the armature slightly. But when I did a tightly bent knee, I ran into a problem with it. It would pop the kneecap off right where the armature was bent. So, when I do a tightly bent knee—if the figure is kneeling down or something—I have to bend the armature well back of the knee. I actually make two bends where the knee should be, so that there is a lot of Sculpey ahead of it and it won't pop that kneecap off.

Q: When you have a larger head made of Super Sculpey, it tends to become very heavy. For digitizing models this is okay, but what about putting this heavy a head on a body?

RC: I have heard of using urethane foam as a core to alleviate the weight. I use it for my accessories and it can be baked, unlike Styrofoam. Styrofoam is a no-no and can give off poisonous gas.

JC: That's why some artists who are doing the bigger heads are going to Paperclay. It's lighter, but Paperclay does not have the look of the polymers at all. The polymer sculptures tend to have more life to them, while the Paperclay looks more opaque, so they don't have the life to them.

Q: What do you use for fingernails, toenails, and teeth?

JC: I sculpt everything. Glass eyes are wonderful to use and there're all kinds of wonderful glass eyes available, but I sculpt the eyes. I sculpt the fingernails with the tool Richard made for me, making a little indentation where the nail bed is and then adding a little flat piece of Super Sculpey over the top and push it in just to give myself a fingernail, and then draw the nail line across and it works out great. I sculpt my teeth right in the mouth. Some people sculpt dentures. They literally make the dentures and stick them right into the head before it's baked. I like to sculpt mine right in the head because I'm always changing it.

Q: So you use Super Sculpey for the teeth?

JC: Yes. I paint them when I'm done. I keep the teeth smooth enough to paint a nice polished finish on the teeth; that is the one area [where] I will use the acetone for smoothing. I will come in with my real fine (five hairs) brush, dip it ever so slightly in the acetone, and that cleans it up really, really nice. Afterward I paint them and then cover the teeth with several thick coats of high-gloss medium. That gives it that shiny look a tooth will have.

Q: As members of the world of original doll art, what do you think is the direction of this sculpting field?

JC: I think the doll world is going in a very exciting direction. It will get more and more creative. I think it will explode with imagination. You can see it just in the time we've been in it. It's jumped by leaps and bounds.

RC: But there has to be more awareness about what this art is. It's a fine-art medium that people have to become aware of. People still have that stereotype in their minds when you say "doll," and they don't picture accurately what we do.

JC: That's what's going to be necessary to keep the doll world alive, to let it now go into another direction. Just like anything, it has to grow and go in new directions to keep it and the art alive and exciting. It's going in new directions, like the computer world. There are so many people who sculpt so wonderfully, but they are limited by their thinking. If they'd only think of new directions to go with it, it opens up a new world.

In The Next Chapter

In Chapter 4, we'll create an armature and sculpt a head step by step with Super Sculpey. You'll see many of the techniques illustrated that were discussed in this chapter. So get your Super Sculpey and your tools—the next chapter is hands-on!

Chapter 4

Sculpting the Basic Head

Chapter Objectives

- Learn to make a basic head armature.
- Learn to add facial features.
- Learn to choose eye types.

In previous chapters, we covered the basic tools and clays used in sculpting and learned some tricks of the trade from other sculptors. In this chapter, I take you step-by-step through techniques for actually sculpting a clay head. We'll sculpt a 2-inch head with Super Sculpey to use on a maquette figure; but keep in mind that the same techniques shown here can also be used to sculpt in larger scale for digitizing models. Once your creation is sculpted, you can change the basic head and features to create any type head you desire—for instance, an alien. First knowing how features relate and are placed on a realistic human head will give you a visual base to work from.

Getting Started

As mentioned in Chapter 2, planning is everything. If you don't have a specific head in mind and you're not working from drawings or pictures to reproduce an existing character, you have a little more freedom to forge ahead and watch as the character is "born." But even then, you should ask yourself some basic questions before embarking on the actual sculpting process:

- Will this model be used for maquette or digitizing?
- Will the model be sculpted on a small or large scale?
- Is it a humanoid, insect, or some other creature?
- Will the sculpted head be attached to an armature? If so, will I use metal tubing or a wooden dowel to attach it?
- What type of clay is best for this application?

- If I'm using an oven-baked clay, will my finished model fit into my oven?
- Will I use glass eyes or sculpt my own?
- Will the finished model be painted?
- If I'm creating a maquette, what pose do I want? Will the character be holding something in its hands?
- Will it be a caricature or a realistic figure?
- Is my character of a specific nationality or race?

All these questions must be answered before the actual sculpting can start. Often in the workplace, most are answered by the design supplied to you, the sculptor, before you begin. The technical details on construction, however, will be left to you.

In this exercise of sculpting a head, the following tools and materials are required:

- A one-pound box of Super Sculpey.
- A wooden dowel with a circumference of $1/4$ inch and a length of 3 inches.
- Aluminum foil.
- Hot glue (hot melt, not cyanoacrylate).
- A penny.
- An orange stick (found at beauty supply stores). This tool is cheap and versatile, but if you want, you might also be able to obtain used dental spoons from your dentist.
- Small paintbrushes ($1/4$-inch flat and smaller will do for this size head).
- Sculpting stand (small block of wood with $1/4$-inch hole for dowel to fit).
- Glass or plastic eyes (optional). For a 2-inch-high head, use 6mm glass, if available. Choose eyes with *irises* that are sized to match the head you will be creating. If ordering from a catalog, you might not be able to see the iris size; in that case, stick with 6mm for a 2-inch-high head, 10mm for a 4-inch-high head, and so on.

TIP

HANDLING OIL-BASED CLAYS

Super Sculpey and most of the other low-temperature synthetic clays are oil-based. As you work with clay—hold it in your hands, knead it, use your fingers to smooth it—the oil from the clay has a tendency to get on your skin. From there, it's easily transferred to furniture, clothing, hair, glasses, and so on. While this isn't a health hazard, it can be annoying. Wash your hands often.

Cleanliness is vital when working with Super Sculpey. Like all clays, it picks up dirt, dust, and hair, producing a surface that can be rough and discolored. Don't rest your soft sculpture directly on any surface, no matter how clean it looks, and stay far away from newspaper!

Other tools you might consider using while sculpting:

- Reference model of a human skull, human ear, hand, foot, and so on. Real-life models are easier to translate to clay sculpture than a diagram or picture.
- Pictures of faces from books and magazines.
- A mirror to use your own features as reference.

After you've answered all the questions listed previously and collected your materials, you're ready to start sculpting.

The Head Armature

The technique for making the head armature is one I've been using for quite some time, and it has never let me down. For this basic head, a wooden dowel is part of the armature. It's easy to hold onto as you work and will easily attach to a body armature later.

> **TIP**
>
> **USE A STAND**
>
> You will probably find that a stand is absolutely necessary to sculpt heads over 3 or 4 inches high. At that size, it becomes too difficult to hold the head in your hands as you sculpt without moving the clay accidentally while you work. The larger the head, the more substantial the stand must be.

As shown in Figure 2-14 of Chapter 2, an armature stand is used to store the head as well as to hold it as you work. It also works well to hold the head up in the oven as it bakes.

To construct the armature:

1. Place the wooden dowel in your armature stand and lay the penny flat on the top, as shown in Figure 4-1.
2. Cut several round pieces of aluminum foil, approximately 4 to 5 inches in diameter.
3. Take one round of aluminum foil that you cut in step 2, and wrap the penny on the wooden dowel as shown in Figure 4-2. Squeeze the foil down securely, eliminating any air bubbles.
4. Cover the top of the foil-covered penny with hot glue and continue down the side, as shown in Figure 4-3.
5. Crumple up a small ball of aluminum foil approximately 1 inch in diameter and place it on top of the hot glue, as shown in Figure 4-4.

Figure 4-1 *A penny has been placed on the wooden dowel so that the dowel won't work its way through the clay as you sculpt.*

Figure 4-2 *The penny and dowel have been wrapped with a round of aluminum foil, holding the two parts together.*

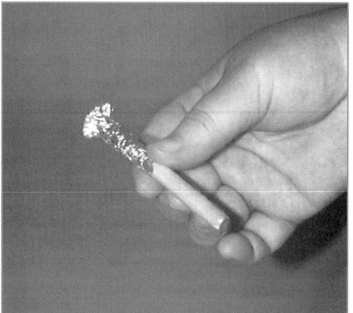

WARNING!

Be careful not to touch the glue while it is hot. It will burn your skin.

Figure 4-3 *Hot glue is applied on the covered penny and around the sides to hold more foil in place. The hot glue will also remelt at baking time to ensure thorough baking of the clay.*

Figure 4-4 *The ball of aluminum foil acts as lightweight filler for the inside of the clay head.*

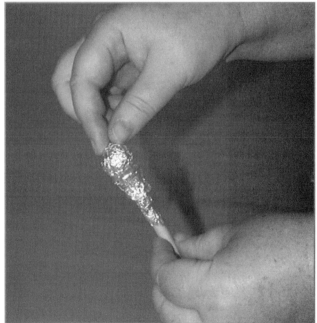

6. Cover the aluminum ball with two or three more layers of aluminum foil, as shown in Figure 4-5.

You now have a basic structure to work from. The aluminum foil will create a lightweight interior for the head and the hot glue will reliquefy as the head is baked, allowing the clay to cook from the inside out as well. The hot glue will also fill any air bubbles left in the foil.

Figure 4-5 *The armature is now ready for the clay to be applied over the aluminum foil.*

> **TIP**
>
> ### WORKING THE CLAY
>
> You must "condition" the clay by kneading it before you apply it to the head. However, if you overknead the clay, it may trap air bubbles, which will cause the clay to crack while baking. To avoid this, simply roll the clay in your hands to warm it. Doing so makes it soft and more pliable to use. If you apply the clay to your sculpture without conditioning it, it may produce undesirable results, like cracking, flaking, or poor adhesion.

Creating a Basic Head

At this point, you have an armature that will carry the weight of the clay you'll be applying. This is only one method of making such armatures; if you have a favorite type of armature that's different from the one described above, you're free to use it. At this point, you should have the armature ready to receive the clay.

Now we're ready to apply the Super Sculpey to the armature. The basic head is the first shape we create as a base for our facial features.

To sculpt the basic head:

1. Wash your hands.
2. Roll a marble-sized piece of Super Sculpey in your hands to soften it. Flatten the ball out.

TIP

STARTING WITH A SKULL

Richard Creager (see interview in Chapter 2) suggests that you first try sculpting a skull before you actually start sculpting a head: "It really gives you a good indication where the facial structures are, and once you've sculpted a skull, the structure is ingrained in you as you sculpt every head thereafter."

3. Apply the flattened clay to the armature, making sure that you have pressed it on firmly enough to eliminate air bubbles.

 Although you could use a single large ball of Super Sculpey to create the head shape in one step, you run a great risk of creating air bubbles. Always use small amounts and build up the surface gradually.

4. Repeat Steps 2 and 3 as needed to create the basic head shape shown in Figure 4-6.

Figure 4-6 *Flatten the clay and apply it over the aluminum foil until you have a basic head shape.*

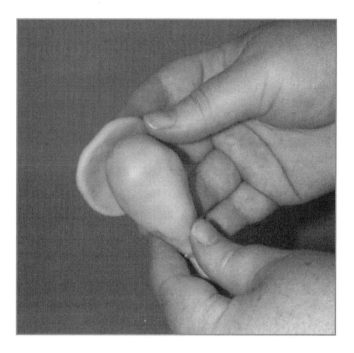

5. After you have covered the entire head area with clay, rub the clay with your fingers to get most of the lumps and bumps smoothed out.

 You can see that this does not look like a human head at this point. We need to add more clay to make the shape of the basic head match that of a human's. Referring to a skull model at this point can be advantageous. Looking from the top, the shape of the skull is basically egg-shaped, with the larger rounded end at the back of the head, as shown in Figure 4-7.

Figure 4-7 *The top view of the skull. The front of the head has a smaller rounded surface than the back.*

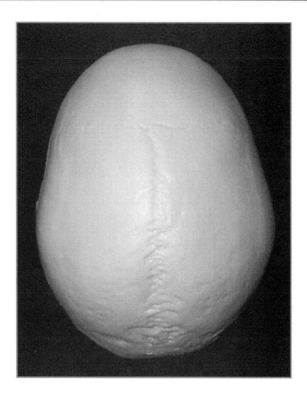

Notice the slope of the forehead in the profile view of the skull shown in Figure 4-8. One of the mistakes most people tend to make when sculpting a head is to make the forehead the wrong size and shape. Inevitably, I have to add more clay to the forehead after I sculpt the features. See the section "Adding More Forehead" later in this chapter.

Figure 4-8 *The profile view of the skull shows the slope of the forehead.*

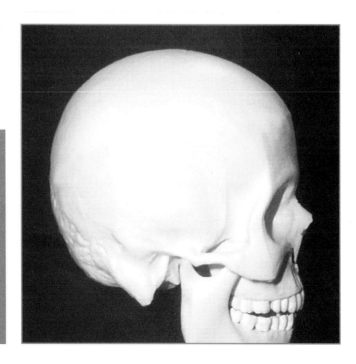

TIP

MATCH THE BASE TO THE FINAL SHAPE

Whenever you're sculpting a head, it's important to have your basic clay head as close to the final shape of your character head as possible.

The last thing to heed as you add clay to your head is the position of the face. The face is formed by adding clay onto the front of the head from the eyebrows to the chin. This gives you more slope to the forehead and, ultimately, makes your wooden dowel positioned to the back of the head instead of sitting in the center, as shown in Figure 4-9.

Figure 4-9 *The profile of a basic clay head before facial features have been applied and the surface refined.*

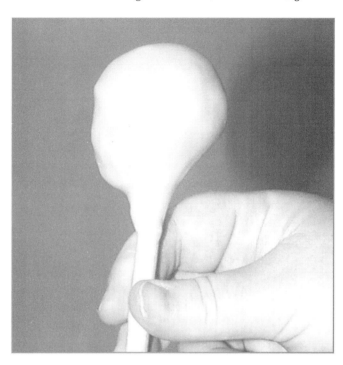

6. Add more clay to flesh out the head. Use another marble-sized piece of clay and lay on the front of the head to provide mass for the face.

7. After smoothing the clay with your fingers, pinch the clay in slightly at the temples with your thumb and forefinger.

Marking Facial Features

Here are some tips to keep in mind when you're sculpting a face:

• Nothing on the face is flat. If you start to get flat-looking surfaces, especially around the upper lip, reshape.

• The face is seldom perfectly symmetrical. To prove this to yourself, try putting a hand mirror along the vertical axis of a face in a photograph. Look at the face formed by half the picture and its reflection. If it's like 99.8 percent of all the faces on earth, it won't look right, because the true alignment is asymmetrical.

• Facial features are not aligned in a straight line. Everything has a curve.

• Everything is connected into a continuous skin. There are no seams in your face, and there should be no seam lines in your sculpture. One part flows into another. This is especially true around the eyes and mouth.

•   The ears are part of the head, not appliances stuck on the sides. Always smooth in their edges to make them a continuous part of the face.

The first thing we do to create a face is to locate and mark the proper positions for facial features, as shown in Figure 4-10. These division lines act as guidelines for feature placement.

Figure 4-10 *The feature lines have been marked on this clay head with wire so you can see them more clearly.*

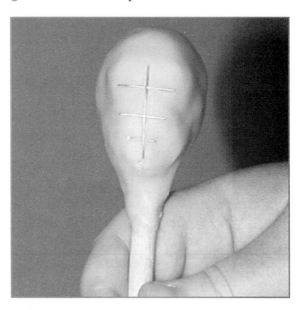

TIP

ADDING A FINGER REST

I'm the worst at wanting to hold the clay in my hot little hands. I just can't stop myself. So I've taken another tip from master sculptors Richard and Jodi Creager. As shown in Figure 4-11, I flatten a small ball of clay and stick it to the back of the head, just where my fingers rest as I hold the head to sculpt. Now, instead of pushing the head of my character around and distorting my hard work, I'm pressing on the pad of clay. When I'm done sculpting, I can just peel it off. Voila! A perfect head.

TIP

LOCATING THE EYE SOCKETS

Your eyes are located on the eye line and they are one eye-length apart.

To mark out the face:

1. Use the pointed end of your orange stick or tool to make a small indentation where the chin will be.

2. Next, draw a straight line from the middle of the forehead to the chin.

3. Halfway between the top of the head and the chin, draw a horizontal line. This line will be the eye midline.

4. Draw two more lines, dividing the area between the eye midline and the chin into three equal segments. The first line under the eye midline is the bottom of the nose. The next line is the mouth line.

These are only guidelines as you begin work on the facial features. The face will change and the lines will fade or be covered as you work, but they will give you a good start.

Figure 4-11 *The pad of clay resting on the back of the head gives your fingers a place to hold the head steady as you sculpt, without damaging the clay head.*

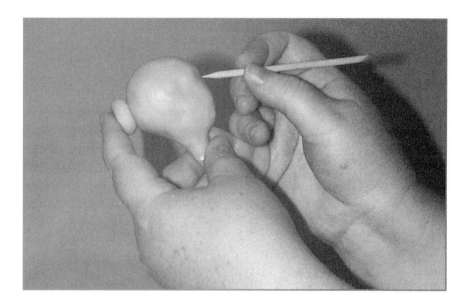

Adding Eye Sockets

The eye sockets are the next things we add to the face to give us a reference as we work.

1.   Press your thumb or finger into the clay in an upward direction where the eye sockets should be. The clay that is moved up from the indentation can be used to form the brow and the orbital bone that surrounds the eye, as shown in Figure 4-12.

Figure 4-12 *Using your fingers to form the hollows for the eyes allows you to push the excess clay up to form the brow and orbital bones at the same time.*

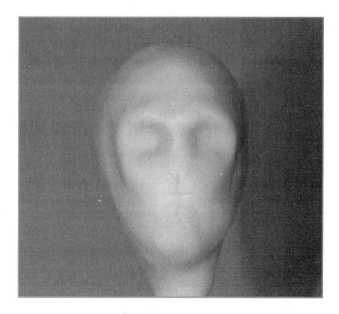

2. Smooth the clay at the bottom of the sockets into the face.

    You can use either glass eyes or sculpted clay eyes. Later in this chapter, we'll discuss both techniques. You can decide which works best for you. (This decision also may depend upon the design and purpose of the head.)

Adding a Nose

I have noticed that when artists start to sculpt facial features, especially the nose, all their work tends to have a vague (and sometimes not-so-vague) family resemblance. We tend to sculpt what we see. Because what we see most often are our families, or even our own reflections in the mirror, those features come out in the clay.

Another phenomenon I've noticed in years of teaching sculpting classes is that a roomful of people can receive exactly the same lesson on how to build a face, but in the end, all heads will have their own personalities and looks. The individual's art always shines through.

Now let's add a nose to the head:

1. Roll a small ball of clay (for this head, roughly pea-sized) into an elongated shape.
2. Place the clay on the face between the eye and the nose lines as shown in Figure 4-13. This will be the base for your character's nose.

Figure 4-13 *The elongated roll of clay is positioned on the face to act as the base for the nose.*

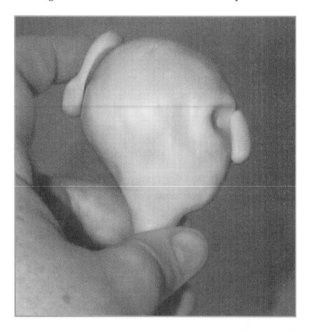

3. With your fingers, smooth the sides of the nose into the face on either side.
4. Smooth the top end of the nose up into the forehead.

    Now we'll put some nostrils in the nose for reference. Remember that the clay will change as you sculpt, and this is only the base of the nose. Once you add the lips and chin to the face, you might find the nose too small or too weakly shaped. In that case, just add more clay to it.

Insert the pointed end of the orange stick (or another pointed tool) into the point where one nostril should be located and gently pull the clay out to the side to form a nostril "wing." Then repeat for the other side to produce the effect shown in Figure 4-14.

Figure 4-14 *The nostrils and nostril wings are formed on the nose.*

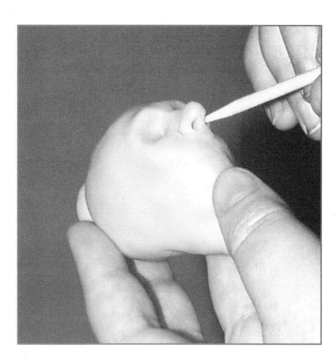

Shaping and Placement of the Nose

Look at a picture of a nose, or better yet, look at your own nose in a mirror. Notice that the nostrils aren't just pulled out to the side; they're angled. You can adjust the angle and size of your clay nostrils as you go along, refining them until they suit you. Note also that the sides of the nostril wings are always curved higher than the mid-area of the bottom of the nose.

Run your finger down the side of your nose; you'll feel that it blends smoothly into the cheek on both sides. Make sure your nose is long enough to allow the sides to blend into the cheeks. Luckily this clay is very flexible: Just pull it gently downward toward the chin to lengthen a short nose. If you need more clay, simply add a little more.

Now that we have a semblance of a nose, we can continue by adding the upper lip.

Adding the Upper Lip

The upper lip says a lot about one's personality. Whether it's a "stiff upper lip" or a full, broad, saline-injected lip like Goldie Hawn's in the movie *The First Wives Club*, it definitely contributes substantially to the look of your character.

1. Shape a $1/4$-inch ball of clay into a fat triangle.

2. Lay the triangle directly under the nose, with the pointed end toward the nose.

3. With your fingers or the flat end of the tool, smooth the outer edges of the triangle out into the cheek area as shown in Figure 4-15. Make sure to leave the bulk of the triangle in the middle.

Figure 4-15 *The upper-lip clay has been placed and the sides smoothed into the face.*

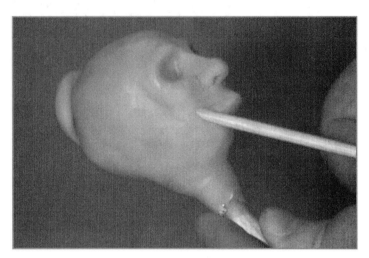

4. With the flat end of the tool, smooth the top of the triangle upward to meet the nose.

   Make sure you don't put a seam or big indentation between the lip and the nose. Also, don't flatten the upper lip as you're smoothing the clay.

5. Smooth the upper-lip edge into the nostrils. Then, laying the tool point-up from the lip to the mid-nostril, push the point under the nose and roll slightly from side to side to place the *philtrum,* the indented fold that runs between the nose and the top edge of the upper lip.

6. With the flat end of the tool, cut a line across the mouth opening to separate the upper lip shape from the rest of the lip, as shown in Figure 4-16. If you have been a little overzealous about smoothing, or if you just need a better shape to your lip, insert the flat end of the tool under the lip, and with the flat side down, lift it slightly.

Figure 4-16 *The upper lip has been defined and the excess will be smoothed into the chin.*

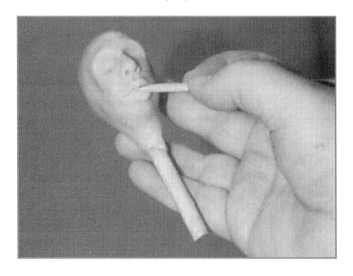

Shaping the Upper Lip

The upper lip has a distinctive wing-like shape. Remember that the surface of the lip is rounded; don't flatten it out.

1. Using the flat end of the tool, place the tool tip where the lip wings will be and roll with the curve of the lip up to form the two peaks on the top edge of the mouth. See Figure 4-17.

Figure 4-17 *The shape of the upper lip and how it blends into the areas surrounding it are essential for a natural look.*

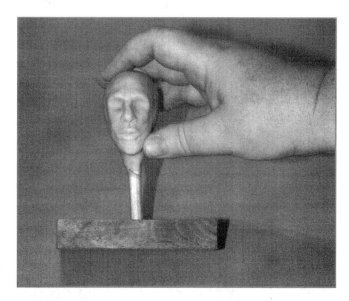

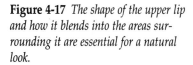

SCULPTING IN SYMMETRY

It's always a good idea to turn your clay head often and look at it from every angle as you add features. This lets you see if your head is adequately symmetrical, if one eye pops out from the head farther than the other, if the nose is straight, and so on. We're not striving for absolute symmetry, just trying to avoid a Hunchback of Notre Dame look.

If you're still having problems determining whether the head is even, look at it in a mirror. The reverse reflection will often help you see any unevenness the naked eye misses.

Another good tip for making sure your head is smooth is to hold it over a black cloth or matte paper and look at the silhouette as you rotate it. This really helps you pick out those little lumps and bumps.

Last but not least, it's always a good idea to sculpt from a profile view. You can readily pick out where the face is incorrect from the side, even if you can't see it from the front view. If you're sculpting a likeness of a person, always be sure to get a good side view. You can't sculpt a good likeness without it.

2. With the flat end of the tool inserted under the lip below each peak, raise the lip slightly so that a slight protuberance is visible in the middle of the upper lip. This is called the *tubercle*.

   Note: The tubercle of the upper lip on a baby is very pronounced.

3. With the edge of the flat end of the tool, make a slight indented line around the upper lip to give the lip some depth.

Adding the Lower Lip

With the upper lip in place, it's time to add the lower lip:

1. Roll a ball of clay large enough to make the lower lip and the chin, approximately 1/4 inch in diameter.

2. Flatten the ball with a straight, rounded edge for the lip.

3. Lay the flattened clay in place and smooth the sides of the chin into the face.

4. With the point of the tool, roll the outside edges of the lower lip under the top lip and pull the clay out a bit at the outside edges of the lip to form the little fat pads that are right at the outside of the mouth on each side. See Figure 4-18.

Figure 4-18 *The lower lip is rolled under the top lip and pulled to the side slightly to form the small fat pads next to the mouth.*

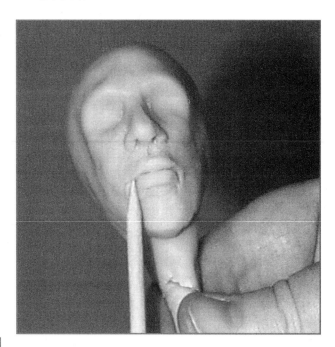

Remember to blend the chin in with the lower lip. The lower lip will curl out slightly over the chin. Don't make it flat or put a seam in it.

5. Place a downward-curved crease in the chin directly under the bottom lip to form the *mentolabial furrow* (the area where the chinbone sticks out farther than the lips).

Now the head is starting to look somewhat human. However, it still has a skeletal appearance; we need to add some more tissue to the face. Let's add the cheeks first.

Adding Cheeks

We can add some cheeks, or even jowls for older characters, by simply adding a little clay.

1. Make a thin roll of clay that extends from the side of the nostril down to the chin, as shown in Figure 4-19. Make sure the roll doesn't come down onto the mouth. This fold, called the *nasolabial fold* or *furrow,* never runs into the mouth, but stays out to the side.

Figure 4-19 *The roll of clay will become part of the nasolabial fold of the face and will add more tissue to the face.*

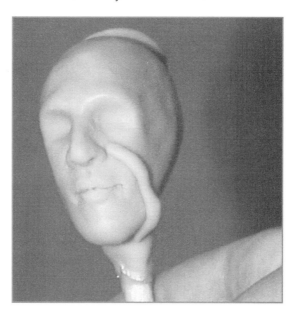

2. After you have the roll properly placed on the face, use the side of the tool and roll the face edge of the roll toward the cheek. Leave the rolled edge toward the mouth as is. As shown in Figure 4-20, this gives your character an older look. The younger you want your character to look, the more you should smooth both sides of the fold into the surrounding tissue.

Figure 4-20 *The interior of the nasolabial fold is left as is for an older look.*

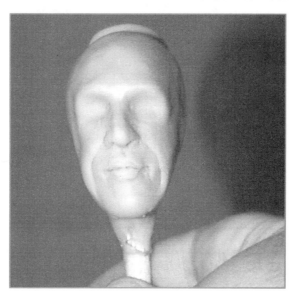

The nasolabial fold can extend down around the side of the jawline to give a jowly look.

3. Roll two pea-sized balls of clay. These will be added to the cheeks.

4. Place the balls on the outside edges of the cheeks below the outer corners of the eyes. Notice that this extra cheek material doesn't go directly below the eye.

5. Smooth the ball of clay into the face, giving it some added bulk, as shown in Figure 4-21.

Figure 4-21 *Extra clay has been added to the outside edge of the cheekbones to give more mass to the area.*

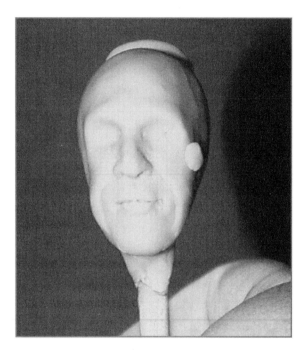

Sculpting Age

Sculpting a head to show age, whether a child or a geriatric, takes some knowledge of *how* we age. Looking at a child's face, with its smooth, rounded shapes, you'd think it would be much easier to achieve that look than that of a craggy old man. Not so. Review Chapter 2 for more insight into the construction of body types.

Adding the Eyes

Now we can add the eyes. Before we choose which technique to use, clay or glass, the structure around the eye socket must be built up enough to house the eye realistically. So before we start, let's take another look at that skull. The bones around the orbits of the eye protrude to protect it from injury. If these bones aren't represented in the structure of the face, the eyes will appear to roll to the outside of the head, making it look unnatural. The clay should be built up to have a ridge around the side of the eye and up into the brow.

If your head doesn't have the orbital ridges represented, use small pieces of rolled clay to build them up.

Sculpting Clay Eyes

Now that the eye has support, let's look at how to sculpt a clay eye.

There are pros and cons to sculpting eyes with clay. The first obvious problem is making the eye appear round in the socket. Second, for maquettes and character figures whose color is important, the eye will have to be painted. Depending on the size of the head and the smoothness of the clay in the eye area, this can be a problem.

Sculpting the eyes also has advantages. First of all, you don't have to worry about buying a correctly sized eyeball. You simply sculpt the eyes to the size required. Also, you don't need to worry about getting the eyes' gaze to match the turn of the head and facial expression. That's all done after the head is finished. (This is great for someone like me who is always changing things at the last minute.)

The sculpted eye technique I use is one that I learned from Jodi Creager. It's an easy and efficient way to sculpt the eyes and lids at once, and the results are great. What more could you ask for?

Note: For these exercises, an additional head was sculpted in a larger scale to allow you to see eye and ear detail more clearly. On this head, I sculpted one eye and used a glass eye for the other.

Now let's look at the basic steps in sculpting eyes:

1. Roll two small balls of clay of equal size. (This will help you to sculpt two eyes of the same size, always a plus in my book.)

2. Elongate one of the balls slightly and place it in the hollow of the eye orbit.

3. With an orange stick that has had the flat end sharpened to more of a point or with a dental spoon (shown in Figure 4.22), lay the stick horizontally with the tip toward the inner eye, press it in at the tip, and rock back gently, releasing pressure toward the outer eye, making a rounded impression.

Figure 4.22 *A dental tool used for shaping the eye. A lacing tool from Tandy Leather is the same shape and also works well. The tip of the tool goes toward the inner eye and is rocked gently to form the rounded eyeball.*

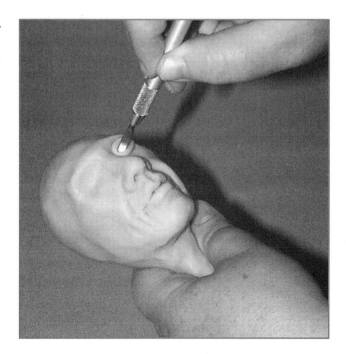

4. Now, place the tip of the tool toward the outer corner of the eye and repeat the procedure in step 3.

    This delineates the lids from the eyeball and produces a basic eye shape to start from, as shown in Figure 4.23.

Figure 4.23 *The rough eye shape that is formed with the rocking of the tool, as described in step 4.*

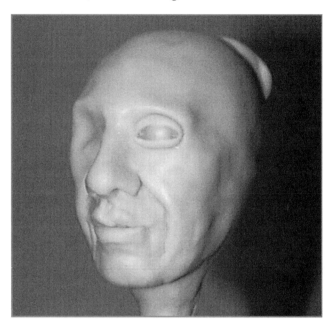

5. Next, take the flat of the tool and blend the excess clay above and below the lids into the face and brow, as shown in Figure 4.24.

Figure 4.24 *The excess clay has been blended into the face and brow.*

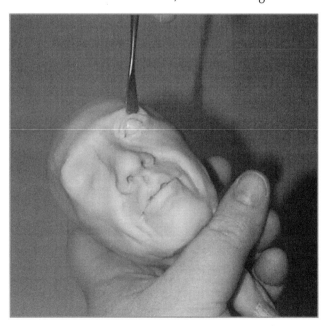

6. Using the flat end of the tool, run the tip under the edge of the lids to slightly separate them from the eyeball, giving the eye more dimension, as shown in Figure 4.25.

Figure 4.25 *The flat of the tool or a dental spoon can be used to separate the lids from the eyeball itself, giving the eye more dimension.*

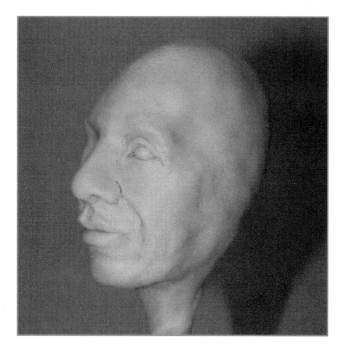

7. Using the point of the tool or a small dental spoon, press into the inner and outer edges of the eyeball to make it appear more rounded.

Eyelid Shape

It's important to know what the shape of the eyes and lids will be before you continue. Here are some important things to know about eyes and eyelids:

- The eyes are set farther back in the head than any other facial feature. All other features are built up from them. The more the features are built up, the more depth to the face. Make sure the eyes don't bulge.

- The eyes don't lie in a straight line across the face: the inside corners of the eyes are on the horizontal midline, but the outside corners of the eyes typically lie a little above the midline. This makes it easy for tears in the eyes to flow down toward the tear ducts. (Racial characteristics can vary this, of course.)

- The outer corner of the upper lid always comes down over the outer lower lid.

- The eye does not sit flatly on the surface of the face. Rather, the lids surround the eye and form to its shape.

- The eyes are one eye-length apart, and the vertical opening of a normally opened eye is usually one-half its length.

- Eyes are also asymmetrical horizontally; that means the upper and lower lids have their own distinct shape. Moreover, the high point of the upper lid does not line up vertically with the low point of the lower lid. The result is that the eye opening is not just a simple oval. Rather, the upper lid is more arched and comes down over the lower lid on the outside corner.

- When a person shuts an eye, the top eyelid seems to do all the work, coming down over the eye and resting on the lash line of the lid below. However, the top lid cannot move without some movement of the bottom lid, even if the lower-lid movement is minute. In fact, the lower lid has a much smaller range of movement than the upper lid. In resting or normal position, the lower lid usually just touches the lower edge of the iris. If a person is crying or laughing, the squinting motion raises the lower lids up much higher to cover part of the pupil from below.

- The lower lid almost never moves *below* its normal position.

- The upper lid in the neutral position lies just above the pupil. If the upper lid touches the pupil at all, the whole look of the eye changes from alert to, well, anything that's not. Since people are all different, the normal position of the upper lid can be considered anywhere from the top of the iris to just above the pupil. However, each eye has its own normal lid position and always returns to it.

Now let's sculpt the eyelid:

1. Shape the eyelids with the tool, making sure they follow the rounded lines of the eyeball underneath.

2. Using the pointed tip of the tool, press in and bring down the inner eye area slightly to form the tear duct.

3. Check the profile to make sure the eyes aren't bulging; if they are, press them in slightly with the flat of the tool.

Using Glass Eyes

Glass eyes have pros and cons just as sculpted clay eyes do. The first advantage is that they can make a sculpted head look alive quickly. Another plus is that they are exactly alike in color, size, and shape and they keep their shape even when the rest of the clay seems to be moving in every direction.

The most obvious problem with glass eyes is their lack of availability. There are several manufacturers from which you can mail order eyes (see the Appendix); however, this takes time and preplanning. Some of the manufacturers carry a wide range of eyes, from beautiful handmade German glass to really inexpensive plastic (great for practice, and, yes, they will bake at Super Sculpey temperatures without melting). Some hobby and craft stores carry a few eyes, too, but they're usually the plastic types.

Another big disadvantage in using glass eyes for maquettes is that eye sizes are usually restricted to 8mm and up, too large for a 12- to 14-inch figure maquette. Some companies do carry small eyes (down to 2mm), but you have to hunt for them. If you don't have them on hand at three in the morning when you've decided *now* is the time to sculpt that head you've been thinking about, you have few options.

One last problem that I hate to bring up but that rears its ugly head (a little pun) is setting the eyes so that both are looking in the same direction. This might seem like a no-brainer, but it's not so when working with Super Sculpey. Even after the eyes have been carefully set into the clay, shifting starts to occur

TIP

PLACING THE EYES FOR FOCUS

If you are sculpting a figure in a motion pose, such as a maquette or character figure, don't have him or her stare blankly into space. If you're doing a digitizing model, it's not a problem. However, a maquette that shows the finished product will lose some of its impact if it's not looking at what it's doing. When the eyes are not pointed correctly, it's immediately noticeable. If someone looks directly at you and then diverts his or her eyes even slightly, you notice immediately. When looking at a near-field object, the pupils of both eyes turn inward until they are directed at the object. The farther the object is from the eyes, the less they must turn inward to focus. Having both irises looking straight ahead produces an unfocused gaze (or that glazed look your teenager gets when you ask, well, almost anything).

as you start to build the features on the face. Soon one eye is looking at the ceiling and the other is looking for loose change on the sidewalk. Some sculptors overcome this obstacle by using a hollow skull as the base of the head. I know of one very well-known, wonderful artist—a perfectionist—who actually carves a hollow skull to match each face. He follows an amazingly complex regimen to allow the eyes to be set into the hollow head after the sculpture has been cured. I don't have the patience to do that.

If you want to use glass eyes, remember to plan ahead and order the eyes you'll need before the sculpting bug bites or the job is due out the door.

Inserting the Glass Eyes

The insertion of glass eyes starts much earlier in the process than is the case with sculpted eyes.

1. After you've marked the head with feature lines (steps 1 through 4 in "Marking Facial Features"), draw a circle on the head where the vertical face line and the eye line meet. Make the circle the diameter of the eyeball you are using.

2. Draw the same size circle on either side of the first, with the sides touching. These will indicate where the glass eyes should be placed.

3. Create the same hollows in the face to allow formation of the brow and orbital bones.

4. With the flat end of the tool, carefully dig out the two circled areas where the eyes will go, as shown in Figure 4.26.

5. Press the glass eyes into the holes and adjust them so that the gaze is correct, as shown in Figure 4.27.

Figure 4.26 *In our one-eyed head, the area for the eye has been carved out to allow the glass eye to be pushed down sufficiently without leaving excess clay to worry about.*

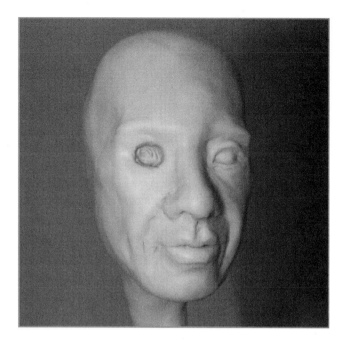

Figure 4.27 *The glass eye has been pushed into position to match the sculpted eye on the opposite side.*

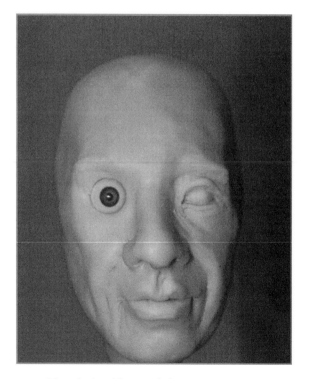

Now let's add some lids.

Adding Eyelids over Glass Eyes

Eyelids are placed over the glass eyes one at a time.

1. Roll a small ball of clay, approximately $1/8$ inch in diameter, and flatten it slightly into a half-circle shape.

2. With the flat side down, place the half circle across the center of the eye as shown in Figure 4.28. The clay should cover the entire upper eyeball and part of the lower brow.

Figure 4.28 *The half circle of clay is placed for the sculpting of the upper lid.*

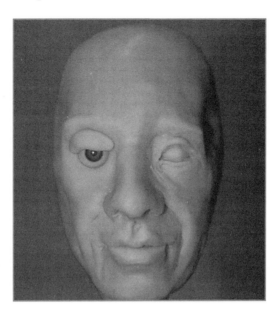

3. With your tool, smooth the upper edge of the clay into the head.

4. With the flat edge of the tool, press into the clay at a perpendicular angle along the surface of the upper eyeball underneath, as shown in Figure 4.29. This makes the eyelid crease.

Figure 4.29 *The flat edge of the tool can be used to create the crease on the upper lid.*

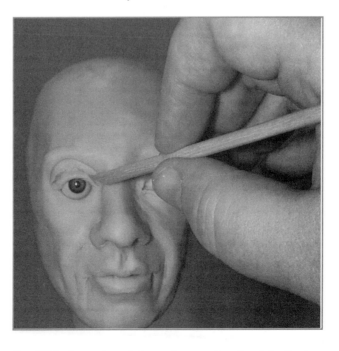

5. With the point of the tool, press the clay into the inner and outer areas of the eye.

Now it's time to add the lower lid.

1. Make another small ball of clay as you did for the upper lid. This time, turn the half circle around, with the rounded area to the bottom of the eye.

2. Lay the clay straight across the bottom of the eye, as shown in Figure 4.30.

Figure 4.30 *The lower lid is created with a half circle of clay placed on the lower part of the eye.*

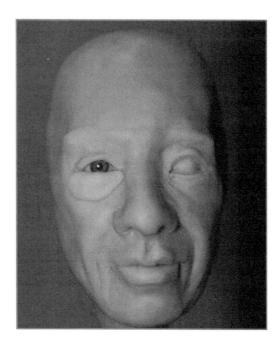

3. Using the flattened edge of the tool, make the crease along the lower lid. Excess clay below the lid can be smoothed into the face or used for bags on older characters.

4. Using the tip of your tool, roll down the clay in the inner corners of the eye to shape the lids. Don't forget the tear duct. As shown in Figure 4.31, the upper outer lid comes down over the lower one, just as with the clay eye.

Figure 4.31 *The eye as it looks after lids have been applied.*

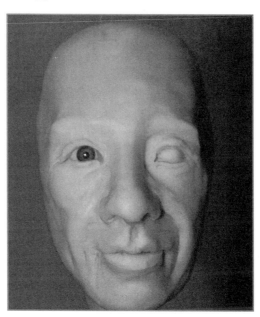

TIP

ADDING MORE CLAY WITH GLASS EYES

You might find the clay eyelids becoming thinner as you work them. If this happens, simply add more clay to build them back up. Also, you might find it harder to build the brow area with glass eyes because you've removed the excess material and added the lids individually. If you see that the space between the eyelid and the brow is too deep, don't be afraid to fill it in with more clay.

Bring your finger up to the inner corner of your eye and notice that there is a small space between your nose and your eye. Don't bring the inner corner of the eye too close to the nose. Also, notice that the area directly above the inner eye has a deeper hollow under the brow. As you move toward the outer eye, the area beneath the brow becomes much more pronounced. In some faces, it will cover the outer upper lid completely.

Sculpting around a glass eye is very similar to sculpting with clay eyes. The advantage, of course, is that the sculpting tools can't affect the glass eye as the surrounding structure is being shaped. However, the basic muscle structure of the eye area remains the same whether you're sculpting with glass or clay eyes.

Now let's use a fat pad to give the eye some character and bring out that outer brow area.

Making a Fat Pad Over the Eye

Most people have a fat pad that lies in the area directly below the brow and over the upper lid at the outer edge when the eye is open. In some people this can droop more noticeably than in others, either from age or just from the way their eyes are structured. To add this fat pad:

1. Make a small, flat circle of clay approximately $1/4$ inch in diameter.
2. Curl one edge under just a bit to give a nice, smooth, rounded edge. This is the side that will be against the eye. Lay the piece of clay over the outer upper lid and brow area.
3. Blend it in just as you did for the nasolabial fold, leaving the rounded edge as is, as shown in Figure 4.32. For a younger look, simply blend more of the pad into the face.

Figure 4.32 *The fat pad has been blended over both eyes to show the effect.*

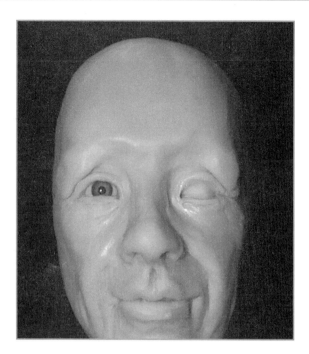

Making Wrinkles in the Face

Now let's add some wrinkles to the sculpted face.

1. At the outer corners of the eyes, make indentations with the side of the pointed end of the tool. Curve these lines slightly upward.

2. Make downward lines from the outer corners of the eyes.

3. Make slight indentations on the eye fat pad and small crosshatched lines on the cheeks.

4. After you have wrinkled your figure, take a small brush and smooth the lines slightly so they won't appear harsh, as shown in Figure 4.33.

Figure 4.33 *Wrinkles have been added around the eyes.*

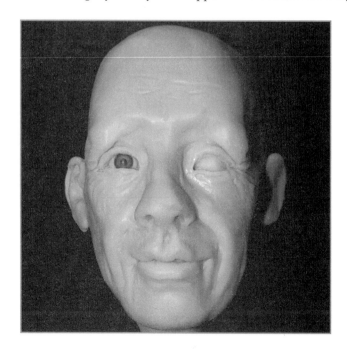

> **TIP**
>
> ## SCULPTING WRINKLES
>
> Wrinkles add character to aged figures. However, wrinkles can also detract from an otherwise good sculpture. The same elements that cause skin spots and sagging also help the skin form noticeable wrinkles in the face, arms, and hands. Wrinkles begin as laugh lines around the eyes and mouth, but with age, they become more permanent and widespread.
>
> Wrinkling is usually most marked in the mouth, eye, and forehead areas where expression, and consequently flexing, is greatest. These are the areas where the skin is stretched and relaxed repeatedly as expressions change. Wrinkling does not always have to be represented by large rolls of skin or heavy, deep lines. This is a mistake many first-time artists make when sculpting wrinkles and folds. Sometimes wrinkling appears on the skin only as delicate hatch marks or crisscross lines. This is most often apparent on skin that isn't pulled and folded onto itself as much with expression changes. Skin on the cheeks is a common area where these hatch marks appear.
>
> Vertical lines that deepen with age also appear around the lips. You've seen them, I'm sure, on elderly women whose lipstick just doesn't seem to stay within their lip lines anymore. Last but not least, the neck often also shows lines and creases with age as the skin loses its elasticity.

Note: Look at photos of older people to see where wrinkles appear on their faces. If you're sculpting more than a head, be sure to include the wonderful wrinkles and lines that appear on an elderly person's neck and hands.

Adding More Forehead

It always happens: As I sculpt, somehow the forehead seems to become more and more sloped as I smooth the clay into the face. If this happens to you, there is an easy answer. Simply add more clay to form the perfect head shape after the features have been sculpted. The easiest way to do this without damaging the work you've already done is to refrigerate the head before adding and smoothing in more clay. This stiffens the clay in the head and makes it easier to work with. Also, keep the pad of clay on the back of the head you've been using as a finger rest, so that as you smooth the forehead, you don't disfigure the rest of the head.

1. Roll a ball of clay approximately $1/2$ inch in diameter.

TIP

SCULPTING ETHNIC FACES

Our world is composed of many varieties of people with varying bone structures, skin, and hair types. When sculpting a character, you must follow the correct racial types to ensure natural-looking results.

Listed here are four of the major types of faces you'll encounter. However, remember that these are only guidelines; each individual is unique. Each of these basic types encompasses a wide variety of peoples. Researching the exact look you want in your character is always advised.

Caucasian

The Caucasian race is usually referred to as white or having a light skin tone. Eye and hair color can both vary greatly. Hair texture is usually described as wavy, but in fact the hair can be anything from stick straight to very curly.

In a side view, the Caucasian head is medium-sized and the chin is usually closer to the spine than is the nose. The Caucasian nose is high and the lips are relatively thin.

African

The African race is usually referred to as black or having a brown to dark brown skin tone. Hair texture is usually more consistent than Caucasian and is usually very curly with a woolly texture. The eyes and hair are predominantly dark brown or black.

In the side view, the African chin juts farther forward than the nose, and the nose is flattened. The lips are usually relatively thick.

If you are modeling an African subject, remember that the facial features and angles will make all the difference between a correct, realistic character and simply a generic, Caucasian-like head with dark skin.

Asian

The Asian face is typically known for its distinct eye shape. Eyelids in an Asian may or may not have more of an upward slant toward the outer perimeter of the eye, depending on the subgroup from which the subject comes. The upper eyelid disappears when the eye is open because of the *epicanthic fold,* which overlaps the lower lid slightly at the tear duct and also may overlap the lower lid at the outer corner of the eye.

Another striking characteristic of the Asian eye is the flatness of the orbit area. Because the bridge of the nose is low and the eye itself is prominent in Asians, the dip between the two planes is likely to be slight. It is important to note that usually the eyebrows are also slightly slanted upward and may taper off abruptly at the ends.

Asian skin is usually represented in yellow or brown tones, and the eye color is typically brown. Asian hair is straight and black.

The chin in the Asian face is typically slightly farther forward than the nose, but not as pronounced as in the African face. The nose is low but not flat, and the lips are of medium thickness.

Aboriginal

The Aboriginal face is characterized by the same marked face angle as in the African face—that is, the chin is typically farther forward than the nose. However, the Aboriginal face has a more sloping forehead and receding chin. The brow is protruding, the nose is large and broad, and the lips are of medium thickness.

Aboriginal skin and eyes are dark brown, and the hair is black. Hair can be either straight or curly.

2. Flatten the ball to form a piece approximately the width of the frontal forehead. Usually, the piece doesn't have to be wide enough to cover the entire forehead from ear to ear. Additional clay will be added to fill in the areas to the sides.

3. Align the flattened piece of clay directly above the eyes on the brow, as shown in Figure 4.34.

Figure 4.34 *A piece of clay has been flattened and attached above the brow to extend the forehead.*

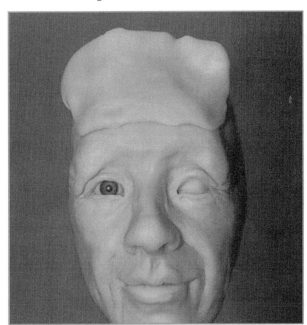

4. Smooth the bottom section into the brow, leaving the top of the flap loose.

5. Move the free flap of clay to form the shape desired for the forehead, as shown in Figure 4.35.

Figure 4.35 *The flap of clay has been formed to the desired shape of the forehead.*

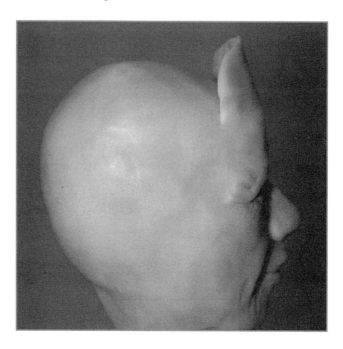

6. Bring in the sides of the clay to make the forehead nicely rounded.

7. Roll some smaller pieces of clay and stick them under the clay flap to fill in any spaces, as shown in Figure 4.36. Make sure the clay fills in all the spaces, and then smooth the flap down to the shape you desire, as shown in Figure 4.37.

Figure 4.36 *Smaller pieces of clay are used to fill in spaces under the flap so that the forehead can be smoothed into shape.*

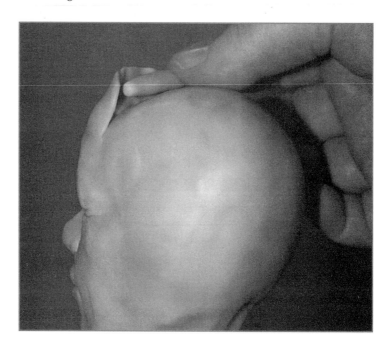

Figure 4.37 *Here are views of the head before (left) and after (right) the forehead was reshaped.*

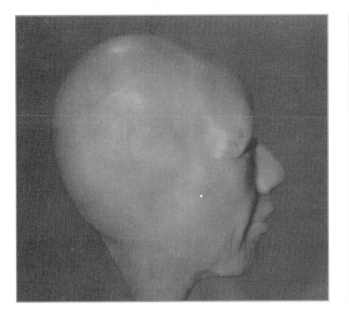
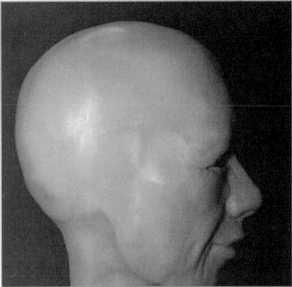

> **TIP**
>
> ## SMOOTHING OUT AIR BUBBLES
>
> Make sure you tap the clay as you smooth to get all the air bubbles out of the clay. If air bubbles are left in, cracking may occur while baking.

Sculpting Ears

The ears are fascinating areas to sculpt. These structures are not only complex, they're also smooth and rounded in a very small area. Some sculptors find this very difficult, especially on a 12- to 14-inch maquette.

Photos, pictures, and drawings of ears can be helpful. However, I find models that can be held and felt in your hands are much more helpful, especially for those of us who are right-brain learners. Looking at the skull model to see where the ear is located is also helpful.

Before you begin to sculpt the ears, keep a few things in mind:

- The ear is positioned halfway between the back of the head and the front plane of the face, directly over the rear angle of the jawbone.
- Generally, with the head looking straight ahead, the ear lies between the top edge of the eyelid and the bottom of the nose.

Now, let's start the ears.

1.   Draw a vertical line on the side of the clay head halfway between the back of the head and the front plane of the face, as shown in Figure 4.38.

Figure 4.38 *A vertical line has been drawn to show the position of the ears on a head.*

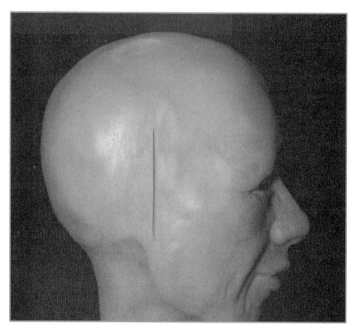

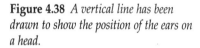

POSITIONING THE EARS

If you nod your head up and down while looking in a mirror, you'll notice that an imaginary horizontal line will shift position with the other facial features. You must always position your sculpted head looking straight ahead to draw the sculpting lines.

2.   Draw horizontal lines across the vertical at the bottom of the nose and the bottom of the brow, as shown in Figure 4.39. This locates the vertical position of the ear.

Figure 4.39 *The horizontal ear lines have been drawn to show the size of the ear and its relationship to the other facial features.*

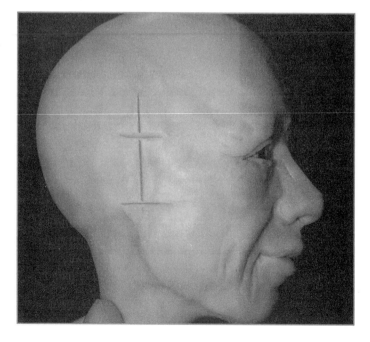

3.   Roll two small balls of clay approximately ¹/₄ inch in diameter. Like the clay eyes, you want to make the ears as close to the same size as possible.

4. Flatten the clay ball into a half circle and then indent it slightly into a crescent shape, as shown in Figure 4.40.

Figure 4.40 *The clay has been shaped to resemble an ear.*

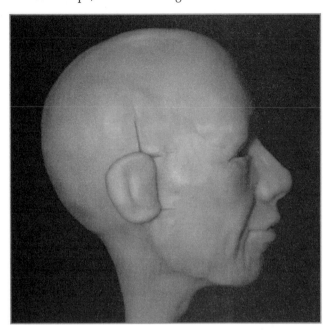

5. Position the clay between the lines you have drawn on the head and smooth the front edges of the ear into the face, as shown in Figure 4.41.

Figure 4.41 *The ear has been placed and the front edge smoothed into the face.*

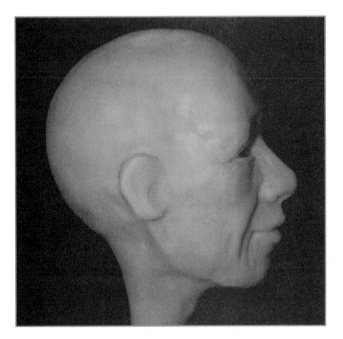

6. Smooth the edges of the ear into the head on the top and bottom so that it is attached firmly to the head.

7. With the point of the tool, make a line on the ear as shown in Figure 4.42. This will be the outer rim of the ear.

Figure 4.42 *The first line drawn in the formation of an ear.*

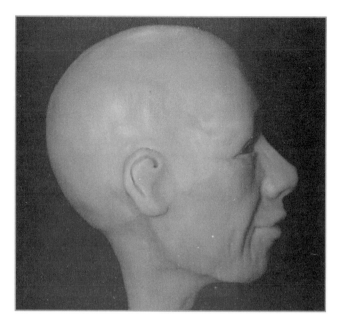

8. Stick the point of the tool into the clay and roll up and down to get the bowl shape of the interior ear surface, where the ear canal will be. Make sure the *tragus*, the little lump that protrudes into the bowl area from the front of the ear, is shaped as shown in Figure 4.43.

Figure 4.43 *The tragus, or the little protrusion at the front of the ear opening.*

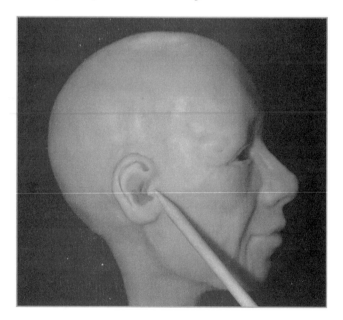

TIP

LINING UP THE EARS

Always look at the head from all angles to make sure the ears line up evenly on the head.

9. Now form the earlobe and the interior cartilage as shown in Figure 4.44.

Figure 4.44 *The ear has been shaped.*

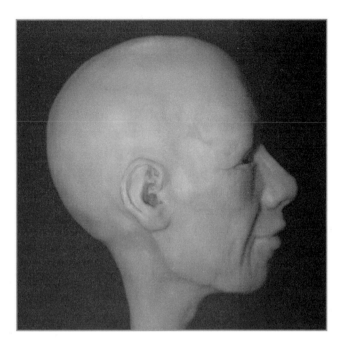

Although you have formed an ear shape, the ear isn't quite complete. If you look at the back of an ear, you'll notice that the ear is held out from the head by the ear structure itself.

1. Roll a small worm of clay and place it behind the ear.
2. Lay the pointed end of the tool along the worm of clay at the top of the ear. Rock gently to press the worm into place as shown in Figure 4.45.

Figure 4.45 *The clay is pressed into place to bring the ear out from the head and give it a natural angle.*

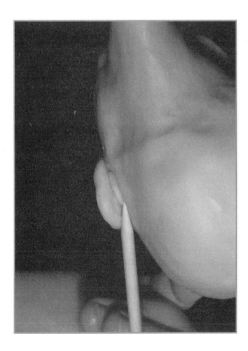

3. Repeat step 2 for the bottom area of the ear back.

4. Repeat steps 1 through 3 for the opposite ear.

After you have applied the ears to your head, go over everything with a small brush and either saliva or acetone to remove any tool marks and make the surface smooth.

Note: If you've used sculpted clay eyes, make sure the surface of the eyeball is *very* smooth so that it will take paint evenly.

In Conclusion

Sculpting the basic head is the first step in creating a character. Human anatomy might not be the look you're going for in your sculpture, but the knowledge of human proportions and anatomy will help you exaggerate the features more easily for a more out-of-this-world look.

In the Next Chapter

In Chapter 5, you will be adding a neck and character to your creation. You'll also learn to bake, paint, and finish the clay. Don't put that head away; we still have work to do.

Chapter 5

Finishing the Head and Adding Expression

Chapter Objectives

- Learn to sculpt the neck.

- Learn to create shoulder plates.

- Learn to add facial expression.

- Learn to bake the clay.

In Chapter 4 we started sculpting a basic head. We'll continue work on the head in this chapter, with the addition of a neck and a facial expression. We'll also fire the finished clay head, and get it ready to be attached to the body.

Sculpting realistic neck and shoulders for your character is never easy. However, it can be much less painful if some basic landmarks, such as the base of the skull and the jawline, are defined before you start work.

Defining the Base of the Head and Jaw

To define these two areas of the head, first take a good look at your own head. This is easy to do with a couple of carefully placed mirrors so you can see the profile. If that's not possible, look at a skull or a picture. As we saw in Figure 4-8, the cranium of the skull (the portion that holds the brain) has a rounded shape. You can see where the base of the head lies by visualizing an imaginary horizontal plane from the bottom of the nose to the back of the head, as shown in Figure 5-1.

1. With the side of the tool laying horizontal along the base of the head, press to make an indention.

2. Work the clay below the line into the neck area.

3. Using your thumb, press into the head under the ear to form the angle of the jaw. The jawline should resemble that in Figure 5-1.

Figure 5-1 *The horizontal plane below the nose shows where the base of the skull lies.*

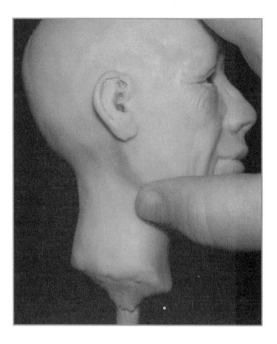

Now that the base of the head and the jawline are referenced, let's move on to the neck.

TIP

HARDENING THE CLAY AS YOU WORK

Often the clay softens in your hands as you work. To keep it hard enough to work with, place it in the refrigerator periodically to harden back up. This will make sculpting much easier.

Adding a Neck

The neck is often sculpted incorrectly. Many times it's created as a straight, stem-like appendage that does nothing more than hold the head off the chest. To note the curve of the neck, look at your own neck in a mirror. Using two mirrors, you can actually see the angle at which your neck projects from the body and attaches to your head, as shown in Figure 5-2. Notice that the neck tilts forward as it comes out from the shoulders. This tilt is usually more pronounced in a woman than in a man because there is less developed muscle in a woman's neck. It's especially noticeable in a weight lifter, a football player, or anyone who has a muscular body type. Because the neck tilts forward, the back of the neck is shorter than the front.

Figure 5-2 *Side view of the neck.*

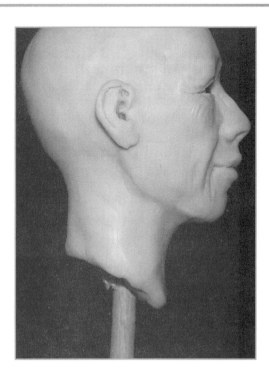

While gazing at a front view of your neck in the mirror, also notice that the sides don't go straight up into the head like a cylinder. As shown in Figure 5-3, the sides taper up toward the head and can vary according to body type and sex. The female neck is usually more slender and graceful than a man's. A man is more likely to have a pronounced Adam's apple.

Figure 5-3 *View of the neck from the front.*

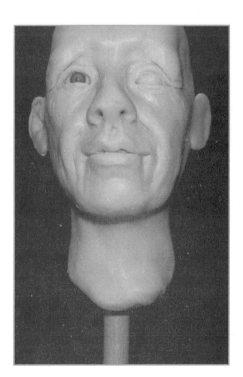

In this chapter we discuss two ways to add a neck to the head. The first is to create a simple neck, which is perfectly adequate for modeling heads that will be used as digitizing models. The second method is useful for making a figure with a non-clay body. This method creates a shoulderplate, which includes the neck, shoulders, and chest area, that can be attached to a cloth body. Sometimes this technique can be useful for maquettes and figures not used for digitizing, when the artist does not need the fine detail of a completely sculpted body.

We'll start with a simple neck for the head we are building. Shoulderplate techniques are discussed later in the chapter.

A Simple Neck

Now let's sculpt a neck.

1. Knead and roll marble-sized pieces of clay and flatten them slightly.

2. Wrap the clay around the wooden neck dowel, pressing tightly as you go to squeeze out any air trapped underneath, as shown in Figure 5-4.

Figure 5-4 *Attaching clay to the wooden dowel to construct the neck.*

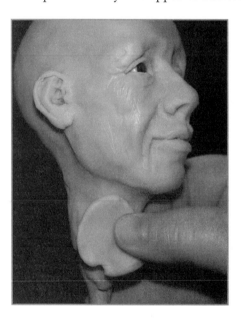

3. Continue to add clay until the neck is the size you desire. See Figure 5-5.

    Note: There are many resource books to refer to when determining the size of the neck. However, looking in a mirror at your own neck will give you a good idea of the relative size of the neck to the head. Turn the head to look at the shape of the neck from all sides. The neck might look perfect from the back and side, but in a three-quarter view, you might be able to see areas where more clay is needed to make it consistent all the way around.

4. Using your fingers, smooth the clay up into the head, making sure the edges are smoothed into the chin and face area and no seams are showing.

    Note: Check the shape of the neck again after smoothing to make sure you didn't alter its shape.

Now it's time to add some anatomy to the neck and base of the skull.

Figure 5-5 *The basic neck shape.*

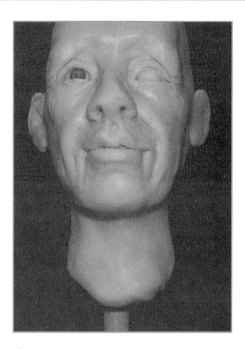

Anatomy

Feel the base of your skull and the mastoid bones behind both ears. You can feel where both sides of the shoulder muscle (trapezius) come up and attach to the base of the skull. Notice the impression or hollow that runs between these two muscles and ends at the seventh cervical vertebrae notch (that small bump on your back at the base of your neck).

1. Using your finger, the back of a large dental spoon, or other small tool, make a slight hollow from the base of the head down the neck, as shown in Figure 5-6.

Figure 5-6 *Make a hollow from the base of the head down the neck.*

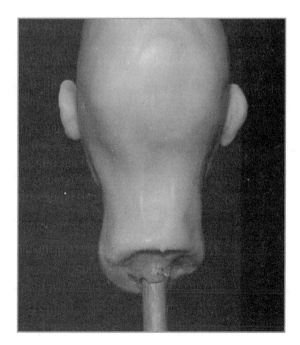

Unfortunately, we all age. If you are adding a little age to your head, a little jowl sag and double chin will do the trick. Let's start the aging by adding a little double chin and sagging to the front of the neck area.

2. Place a ball of clay under the chin, as shown in Figure 5-7.

Figure 5-7 *The ball of clay is placed under the chin.*

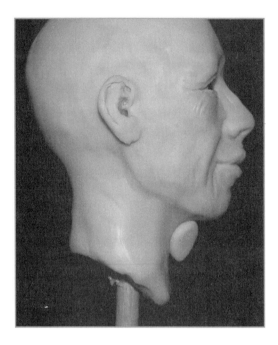

3. Smooth the edges into the surrounding areas, being careful not to smooth away the mass of the clay.

4. Using the flat end of the orange stick or a large dental spoon, place the rounded end into the clay at the left side and roll toward the right, as shown in Figure 5-8. (You used a similar technique when you created the eyes.)

Figure 5-8 *Roll the spoon toward the center to give a rounded look to the double chin.*

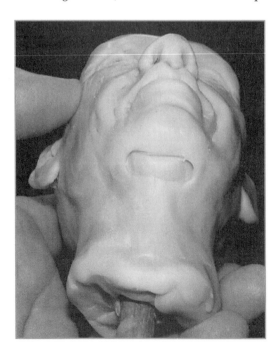

5. Repeat the process on the left side.

   You now have a rounded surface and a sagging side. Smooth the clay around any sharp edges.

6. Take the back of the flat end of the orange stick or the rounded end of a large dental spoon and make an indentation from under the chin down the front of the neck, as shown in Figure 5-9. This creates the "wattle" effect you often see on older people.

Figure 5-9 *Wattles are created by making an indentation from under the chin down.*

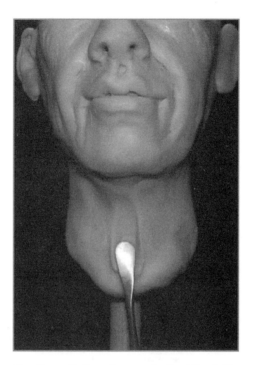

7. Smooth the edges and adjust the folds, as shown in Figure 5-10. (For figures with a younger appearance, the wattle should be minimized or left out altogether.)

Figure 5-10 *The wattles as they appear when done.*

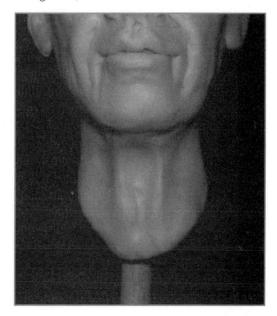

Now let's add the sterno-mastoid muscles.

Adding the Sterno-Mastoid Muscles

The two muscles that have the most to do with the look of the neck are the sterno-mastoid muscles, which come up from the sternum (or breastbone) to below and in back of the ears (mastoid) and the trapezius.

1. Roll a long, thin worm of clay.
2. Lay one end of the worm on the neck behind the jawline and angle it down towards the sterno-clavicular notch, or what is sometimes called the "pit" of the neck, as shown in Figure 5-11.

Figure 5-11 *The clay worm lies on the neck from behind the jawline down to the pit of the neck.*

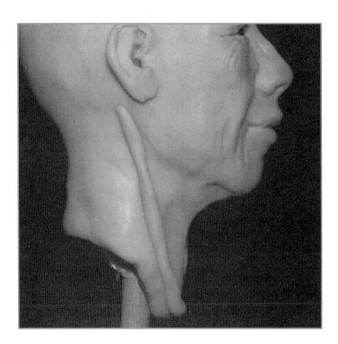

3. Smooth both sides of the worm into the surrounding clay, making sure not to smooth the definition of the muscle away. See Figure 5-12.

Figure 5-12 *The neck as it appears after the sterno-mastoid muscle has been added.*

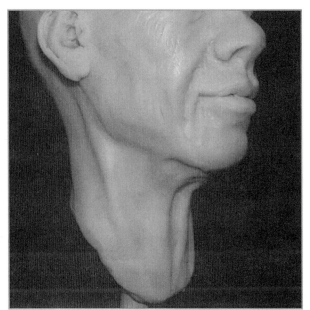

4. Repeat steps 2 and 3 for the opposite side.

Adding an Adam's Apple

If you're looking for that Icabod Crane look, you might want to add an Adam's apple to your figure.

1. Roll a small ball of clay and place it in the V area between the two sterno-mastoid muscles, as shown in Figure 5-13.

Figure 5-13 *The ball of clay is placed for the Adam's apple.*

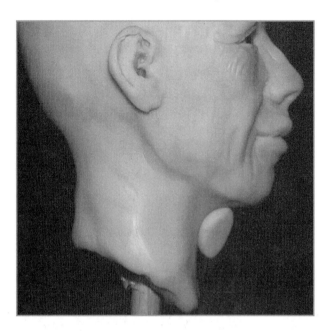

2. Take the small, flat end of the orange stick or a small dental spoon and smooth it into the surrounding clay.

3. Smooth all the clay with a small brush to remove tool marks and finger-prints, as shown in Figure 5-14.

Figure 5-14 *The Adam's apple has been added to the neck.*

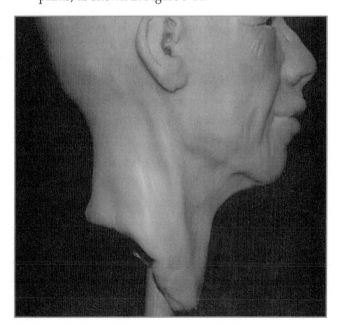

Changing Neck Muscles As the Head Moves

The muscles we have added to the neck appear when the head is in a straight-ahead position. When the head turns from side to side or tilts up or down, the muscles move as well. Some will appear more prominent than others. Here are some tips for sculpting a head turn:

- With the head turned and the shoulders straight ahead, the ends of the sterno-mastoid muscles that attach to the sternum stay in place. The top part of the muscle moves with the head.

- With the head lifted and turned to the side, the sterno-mastoid and clavicles (if you're sculpting shoulders as well) are more prominent.

As you work on the neck, you can remove excess clay with a palette knife or an X-acto knife to keep the edges straight and neat. After the basic neck has been sculpted, you can add wrinkles and creases so it looks like it belongs to the head it's attached to.

Adding Wrinkles and Lines to a Neck

The face isn't the only area where we wrinkle. Age shows on the neck in the look and texture of the skin. By adding fine lines and cross-hatching, you lend age and texture to the skin of your character.

1. Use the flat end of the orange stick and run horizontal lines around the neck. Remember to do this lightly.

2. Add cross-hatch marks at an angle across the horizontal lines to add more texture, as shown in Figure 5-15.

Figure 5-15 *Horizontal lines and cross-hatches appear around the neck to form wrinkles.*

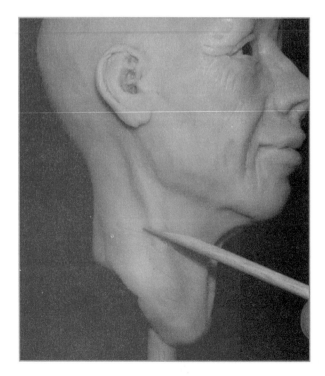

3. After applying the wrinkles, go over the area with a small brush. If you're using solvent, don't use too much, as it will erase small lines and leave you with a smooth, sticky neck.

Now let's look at what's involved in making a shoulderplate.

Creating a Shoulderplate

Adding a shoulderplate to a head can be useful for those who want to make bodies from cloth rather than clay. Using a cloth body provides a lightweight alternative and can be easier to manipulate if the character is to have cloth clothing.

When creating a head that will use a shoulderplate, brass tubing can be used in place of the wooden dowel for the head armature. This makes it easier to pass the tubing through the shoulderplate base and onto the neckwire of the body armature. Here are some tips to keep in mind:

- If you will be using a cloth body, make the body before you sculpt a shoulderplate. It's much easier to fit a shoulderplate to a body than the other way around.

- Use something solid as the sculpting base. I use sheet brass, cut and shaped, to sculpt my shoulderplate on. This way, the clay has something solid underneath and won't crack when pressure is applied to the area. It also holds the figure while I sculpt other parts of the body.

- Draw your shoulderplate pattern on paper toweling before you transfer it to the brass. It's inexpensive and it drapes.

- Remember to make the shoulderplate as large as you need to show exposed chest areas, but don't let it come out over the shoulders so far that it prevents easy application of the arms. If a bare upper body is your choice, the arms can be sculpted onto the shoulderplate section later.

Steps for Creating a Shoulderplate

Now let's see how to create a simple shoulderplate.

1. Create a body that the shoulderplate will fit on. See Chapter 6 for more details on cloth bodies.

2. Cut a piece of paper towel large enough to make the shoulderplate pattern. (For a 2-inch head, cut about a 3-inch square of paper towel.)

3. Cut a slit in the paper towel from an outside edge to the center point, as shown in Figure 5-16. This allows you to slip the paper towel around the neck wire.

Figure 5-16 *A slit in the paper towel has been cut to allow it to come around the neck wire.*

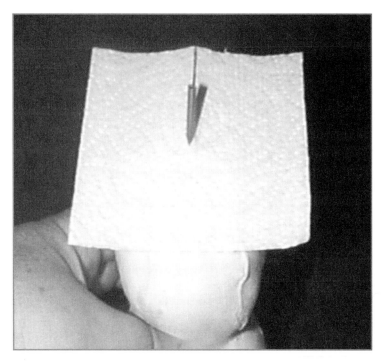

4. Bring the edges together in the back, pulling the bottom edges tighter, until the paper's shape is correct, as shown in Figure 5-17. Pin the edges together and slide it off the neck wire.

Figure 5-17 *Here the paper towel has been drawn around the body into shape.*

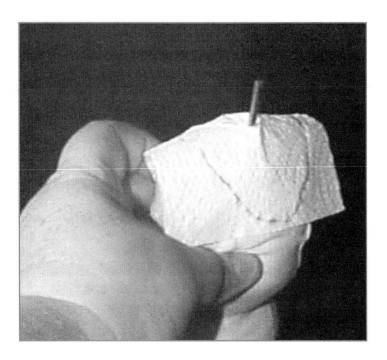

5. Cut off the excess paper. Your pattern edges can now be rounded so the pattern has smooth edges that will blend in easily to the body. See Figure 5-18 for a standard shoulderplate pattern.

Figure 5-18 *A standard shoulderplate pattern.*

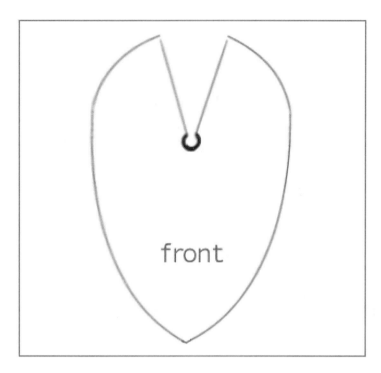

front

6. Using sheet brass thin enough that it will bend, trace your pattern on brass with indelible marker.

7. Using metal cutters, cut the pattern out of brass, being careful not to slice your fingers on the brass edges.

8. Cut a circle out of the middle of the brass shoulderplate to allow the dowel or brass tubing to pass through, as shown in Figure 5-19.

Figure 5-19 *A circle has been cut out of the middle of the brass shoulderplate to accommodate a brass tube used for the head.*

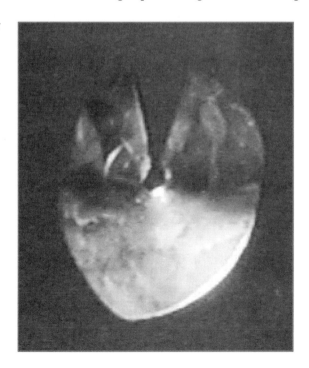

9. Place the brass plate over the cloth body and bend the brass into shape so it fits tightly against the body. Make sure you slide the tubing or wooden dowel (whichever you used on the sculpted head) through the top of the shoulderplate base to make sure it will go on easily. See Figure 5-20.

Figure 5-20 *The brass shoulderplate fitted onto the body.*

Now let's add some clay to the shoulderplate.

Adding Clay to a Shoulderplate

The clay added to the shoulder and chest sections can be much thinner than the traditional simple neck we added earlier. Because of the brass understructure, it has more support. However, applying the clay too thinly can result in cracked or chipped-away clay. For the shoulderplate here, which will go on a 2-inch head, $1/8$-inch clay thickness should give us sufficient support and still blend into the body without a visible ledge.

1. Place the head and shoulderplate together onto the body before you start sculpting, so you can measure the appropriate neck length for your character. This is useful in case the wooden dowel or brass tube is too long and needs to be trimmed to fit onto the body.

2. With the head, shoulderplate, and body still together, add clay to the neck area as we did for the simple neck above. Don't add any additional anatomy yet.

3. Continue applying clay onto the brass shoulderplate, keeping the clay approximately $1/8$ inch thick.

    Note: The clay that's added to the shoulderplate will keep the brass in place, and when cooked, the entire head, neck, and shoulders will be a single structure.

4. Smooth the clay with your fingers until the surface is smooth and all seams where the head, neck, and shoulders connect are invisible, as shown in Figure 5-21.

Figure 5-21 *The neck and shoulderplate have been covered with the basic clay form and smoothed.*

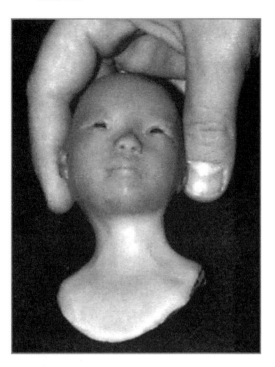

TIP

USING A BAKED HEAD

To keep the clay head from being deformed as you work, you might want to bake the head before the shoulderplate is attached. (See the baking instructions later in this chapter.) If you want to bake your head first, skip to the next section on expressions so you can add personality to the face before it's baked. When adding the shoulderplate to a baked head, make sure to smooth all unbaked clay edges into the baked surface with a brush so no seams will be visible.

Now let's give the shoulders some definition.

Shoulderplate Anatomy

Shoulderplates have the same neck anatomy as the simple neck above; however, since the shoulders and chest are also sculpted, you can now continue the anatomy to include the clavicles and the sterno-clavicular notch.

1. Add the same neck anatomy you used for a simple neck earlier in the chapter.

2. Make two flattened balls of clay, about the size of a small pea, and place them at either side of the midpoint of the chest, as shown in Figure 5-22. These will be the clavicles (collar bones).

Figure 5-22 *Two flattened balls of clay are shown placed for the clavicles.*

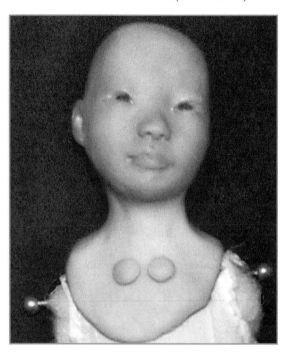

3. Pull and stretch each clay ball up and out toward the shoulder to form the plate that is the clavicle. Make sure to angle the end up slightly toward the top of the shoulder, as shown in Figure 5-23.

Figure 5-23 *The clavicles are angled up toward the shoulder.*

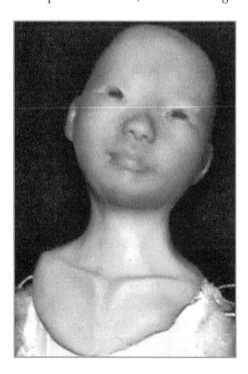

Note: The sternum is the only area where the clavicles are in a fixed position. With up-and-down or inward movement of the shoulders, the outer points of the clavicles can move several inches.

4. For older figures, make the pit of the neck (the little indented section where the two sterno-mastoid muscles meet at the front base of the neck) a little deeper.

5. Smooth clay into the surrounding areas, keeping the clavicular shape intact.

6. Smooth all areas with a small brush. If you used a prebaked head, make sure to brush the areas of unbaked clay into the baked surfaces so no seams show.

7. Take the clay head, neck, and shoulderplate off the body carefully and place it on the sculpting stand.

Now let's add some expression to the face.

Expression

Digitizing models are usually created in a neutral position with a blank expression on the face and the mouth slightly open to allow the lips to be digitized separately. This pose makes it a much easier task to set points and digitize the head into the computer. This is great for a digitizing model because, of course, the character can be brought to life in the computer. For maquettes and sculptures that will show the real personality of the character, however, expression must be sculpted in the clay.

The most important thing to remember when adding facial expressions to your clay head is that facial muscles are all connected. When you smile, more than your lips move. Your cheeks swell, your eyes squint, and your eyebrows raise. A simple movement affects the entire face. The good news is that Super Sculpey is so pliable, it allows us to simply move the face with our fingers and tools to achieve any expression we desire. Now let's give that face a happier look.

Creating a Smile

The smile is controlled by just two muscles: the *zygomatic major*, which pulls on the mouth, and the *obicularis oculi*, which narrows the eye. Even the faintest of smiles will trigger these two muscles.

The more you smile, the more the eye squints. The lower lid bulges, shortens, and rises up on the eye, covering part of the iris. On a laughing face, the eye is closed more from below, with the lower lid meeting the upper lid halfway, higher than when the eye is closed normally. This makes the lash line appear straight rather than curved, as it is when the eye is closed normally.

Crow's-foot wrinkles may appear from the outer eye corner, and laughter may even cause wrinkles to appear from the inner corner. The cheeks swell and tighten, forming an apple shape centered at the nostrils. Dimples may appear at the base of the ball shape of the cheeks. The more relaxed mouth stretches the skin up high on the teeth as it's pulled out and up, and sometimes the gums may also show. The chin drops down and back, forming folds between the chin and neck. On a laughing face, the mouth is more stretched, thinning the lips, particularly the upper lip. There is no movement above the brow line, so the forehead stays relaxed and smooth. Now let's make the head happy.

Sculpting a Simple Smile

Let's start with a simple smile.

1. Using the tip of the orange stick, pull the sides of the mouth slightly up and out to the side, as shown in Figure 5-24.

Figure 5-24 *The face is pliable and can be stretched with the orange stick to achieve a smile.*

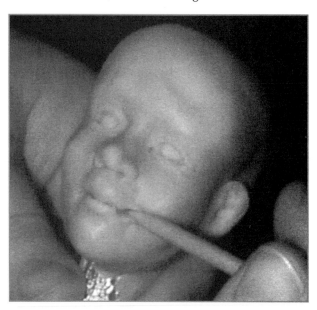

2. Push the cheeks up slightly with your fingers and do the same with the brow areas of the face, as shown in Figure 5-25.

Figure 5-25 *The cheeks and brow have been slightly lifted into a smiling expression.*

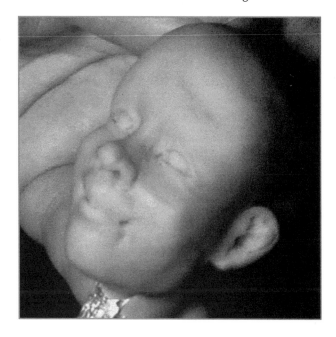

3. Using the flat end of the orange stick, make the lower eyelids bulge upward in a slight arc, as shown in Figure 5-26.

Figure 5-26 *The lower eyelids are brought up slightly in the center to form a smiling eye.*

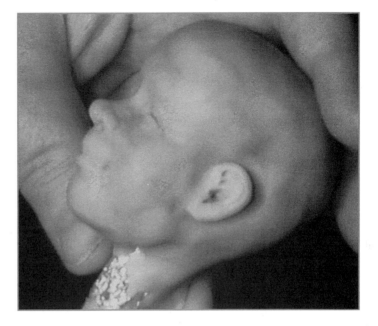

4. Wrinkles can be added to the outer edges of the eyes, and dimples can be added in the cheek area.

Now the head is smiling with its lips closed, as shown in Figure 5-27. Next, we'll open the mouth and show a few teeth.

Figure 5-27 *The final smiling face.*

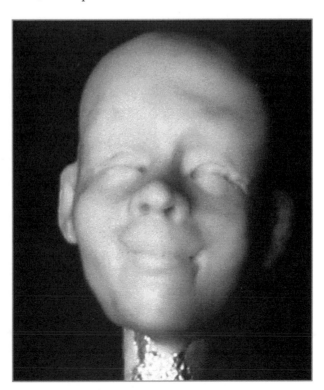

Sculpting an Open-Mouth Smile

In order to have teeth showing, the mouth has to be opened so that the teeth can be sculpted.

1. Using the flat end of the orange stick or a dental spoon, stick the tool between the lips and push down, as shown in Figure 5-28.

Figure 5-28 *The mouth has been opened with an orange stick.*

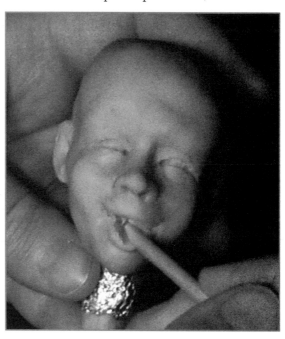

> **TIP**
>
> ### SHOWING GUMS
>
> If the smile will be big enough to show gums, you can sculpt them into the teeth by simply bringing a small amount of clay down from the mouth and arching the gums around each tooth with the pointed end of the tool.

2. Slide the tool to either side of the mouth and repeat until the mouth has been opened wide enough to sculpt teeth, as shown in Figure 5-29.

Figure 5-29 *The mouth as it appears ready for teeth.*

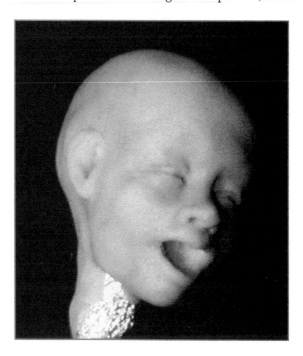

3. Carve out some of the clay inside the mouth to make room for the teeth.

Usually an open-mouth smile (that isn't a laugh) shows only the top teeth.

1. Roll a worm of clay large enough to form the top teeth. In our 2-inch head, that would be approximately $1/4$ inch long.

2. Lay the worm of clay along the top of the mouth, far enough back into the mouth to allow for the fullness of the lips, as shown in Figure 5-30.

Figure 5-30 *The worm of clay is in position for the upper teeth.*

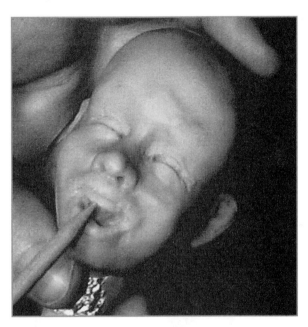

3. Smooth the edges into the mouth, leaving the raised area for the teeth.

4. Using an X-acto knife, slice the ridge of the clay in the center to form the space between the front teeth, as shown in Figure 5-31.

Figure 5-31 *An X-acto knife is used to separate the teeth.*

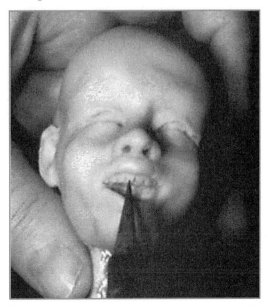

Figure 5-32 *The finished open-mouthed smile.*

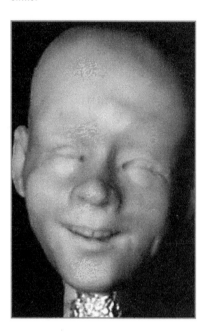

5. Make the spaces for the other teeth, remembering that the front teeth are somewhat larger. For this smile, you won't be able to see much definition between sizes and shapes of the other top teeth.

6. After shaping the teeth, close the mouth back down to the desired position.

7. Make sure the rest of the face matches the expression you have in your smile, as shown in Figure 5-32.

Now let's give the head an open-mouth laugh.

Sculpting an Open-Mouth Laugh

Because we are able to see inside the character's mouth when it is laughing, you will need to sculpt a mouth cavity, upper and lower teeth that are the appropriate thickness, and a tongue.

1. Open the mouth up as you did in the last exercise.

2. Carve out the interior of the mouth, including the interior roof and a space to place a tongue, as shown in Figure 5-33.

Figure 5-33 *The interior of the mouth carved out for an open laugh.*

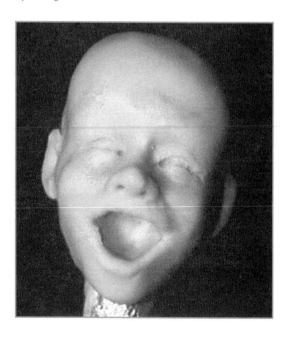

3. Roll a small ball of clay, about $1/4$ inch, and flatten it slightly into an ellipsoid.

4. Place the clay ellipsoid into the mouth for the tongue. The tongue will be enclosed by the bottom teeth.

5. With the point of the orange stick toward the back of the mouth, lay the stick down in the middle of the tongue and gently roll to indent the center of the tongue slightly, as in Figure 5-34.

Figure 5-34 *The tongue as it appears in the mouth.*

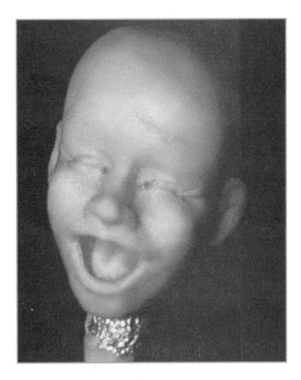

Now we're ready to add teeth.

Realistic Teeth

There are two methods to achieve the look of real teeth: using Super Sculpey sculpted teeth as we did for the open-mouthed smile above; and sculpting the teeth separately from the mouth and inserting them like dentures. The second method is great for realistic-looking teeth for fine-art pieces and for open-mouthed poses like this one.

1. Roll a thin worm of clay approximately 3/8 inch long. This will be the base for your dentures.
2. Flatten the worm slightly and curve it to fit the shape of the upper teeth in the head, as shown in Figure 5-35.

Figure 5-35 *The worm is shaped to fit the upper dentures.*

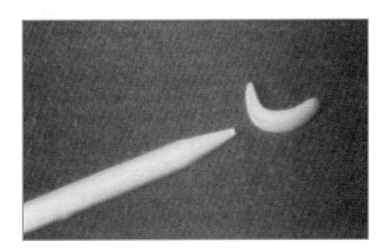

3. When you have the shape right, bake the worm in the oven at 250 degrees for about 10 minutes. If you need further instructions for baking, see "Baking the Clay" later in this chapter.

Now that you have a hardened base to work from, let's make the teeth.

1. Using Super Sculpey or one of the other more translucent clays like Cernit, sculpt the tiny teeth one at a time, judging the size and spacing you need.

2. Press each tooth onto the base, trying not to break the base, as shown in Figure 5-36.

Figure 5-36 *The teeth placed on the denture base.*

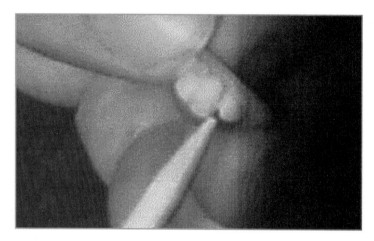

Make sure the front teeth are thicker at the base and thinned toward the end so when the mouth is open, the teeth are sized correctly.

3. After applying the teeth to the base, rebake the entire denture at 250 degrees for 10 minutes.

4. After the denture cools, push the entire piece up and into the top of the mouth, as shown in Figure 5-37.

Figure 5-37 *The teeth are placed in the mouth.*

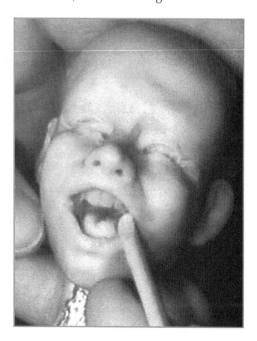

Figure 5-38 *The finished laugh.*

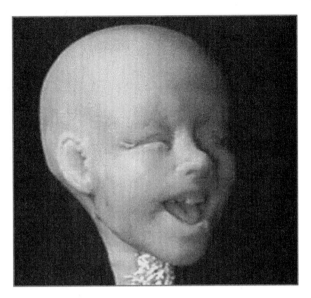

Note: If you want gums to show, clay can be brought down from the top of the mouth to form gums around the teeth.

5. Repeat the above steps for the lower teeth if they will be showing.

6. After the teeth are in place, move the jaw to open or close the mouth into the desired position.

7. Make sure all the surrounding features are adjusted to match the expression.

8. Smooth all areas with a brush to remove any tool marks or fingerprints.

Now let's add some facial hair to the head.

Adding Facial Hair

Facial hair can be anything from eyebrows to beards to eyelashes. In this section I'll explain how to add these to your figure. First, let's start with eyebrows.

Adding Eyebrows

Eyebrows can be either sculpted or painted. I usually scribe the hairs into the clay before I paint if painting is my choice for that character. However, sculpting can give male characters a more bushy, three-dimensional look to the eyebrows.

When applying eyebrows, keep in mind the character's expression. Eyebrows move and react with all the other facial muscles, completing the message you're trying to convey. Remember, all eyebrow movement is from the center of the brow toward the nose. The outer half of the brow stays in place.

Now let's add some sculpted brows to our head.

1. Roll tiny, thin worms of clay.

2. Lay the first roll in position and, taking the flat end of the orange stick, press it into place. Do not smooth in the edges. Continue to lay worms in place until the desired eyebrow is formed, as in Figure 5-39.

Figure 5-39 *The tiny worms are laid into place for the eyebrows.*

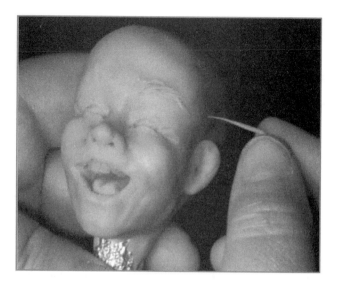

3. Take an X-acto knife and run the tip of the knife along the worm, separating it into thinner strands of hair

4. Add more worms to give a bushier look. The worms can be added on top of the first to give a more haphazard look to the brow.

5. Use the knife to thin the hair strands.

6. Using a small brush, smooth eyebrows slightly.

This method can also be used for mustaches and beards with a fuller look. It allows you to control how the hair lies to give a very refined, groomed look or a craggy, disheveled look.

Now let's look at different types of beards.

Adding Beards and Five-O'Clock Shadow

Beards can be added in much the same way as eyebrows. However, if the beards are long, preplanning is essential. A long, flowing beard needs some base to support it so the strands won't be broken off. However, if you're looking for a short beard that is close to the face, you can add it directly to the head without an underlayment.

Here are some tips to follow when adding a beard:

• Lay the clay in the direction hair would grow.

• Use the X-acto knife to slice the worms into thinner lengths to give the illusion of many fine hairs lying on the surface.

• Apply the clay in layers to build up the thickness of a beard.

• If five-o'clock shadow is what you're looking for, after the clay has been baked, you can stipple the clay with a sharp-pointed object such as an awl.

Now let's look at putting on a head of hair.

TIP

SCULPTING A CREATURE

Up to this point, you have been working diligently on a simulation of a human head. But what if the character you want to produce looks like a dog, a mosquito, or maybe a two-head alien? To produce a character that more closely fits your vision, the basic steps remain the same: You still need model sheets and schematic drawings. You still need an armature that twists together at the spine and foil to bulk up the mass of the body. The biggest change is the shape you start with. For a human head we started with a stick and foil that resembled a Tootsie Roll pop because it most closely resembles the shape of the ultimate head. For a creature with a big snout or large floppy ears, the shape of the base will change to fit the basic structure of the creature.

Creating a Base for a Large Snout

Wrap larger gauge floral wire around the head armature dowel before all the foil is applied. After a base of foil is attached, the wire can be brought out from the head and looped around to the front of the face to form the shape of the snout. Wire is then wrapped around the looped wire to form a cage. Apply foil around the wire before the clay is applied.

Adding Ears

Ears are always at risk of cracking because they stand out from the head. For this reason, it's always a good idea to add some sort of wire structure under the clay. If the ears are very thin and long, a single wire extending from the head armature through the ears might do the trick. But if the ears are wide and floppy, a wire cage like the one produced for the snout might be more appropriate.

Adding Tails, Spikes, and Horns

Tails, spikes on a dinosaur's back, and horns are like ears. They have to have some structure to keep the clay from simply snapping off. Wire can be attached to the twisted wire spine of the armature as the neck wire was, using the $^3/_{32}$-inch bronze brazing rod or brass rod at the position where they attach to the body. This will give you a base to apply foil and clay.

A Head of Hair

Sculpted hair usually looks like Woody's coif in *Toy Story*—that immovable, plasticized look of a cartoon character. Most times these helmetlike additions can be added to your sculpture after the head has been sculpted.

When you're on a job, your creativity might be limited. If this is your own creation, you can consider more options. For digitized models, hair can be left off the clay sculpture altogether. Hair can then be added to the computer model with one of the new hair-generating software packages. Even painting the hair on the final model is an option, though not the most effective one. (Planning rears its ugly head again—this time for hair treatments.) For sculpted models and maquettes that won't be used for digitizing, hair can be sculpted with clay. However, wisps of hair and locks of hair flying in the wind can be broken off easily, because Super Sculpey just isn't that strong. In these cases, the original armature must include a wire form for the hair to give it a strong base. For hair that will lie more closely to the head, sculpting can be done as a last-minute addition. The hair in this case will be sculpted by shaping the overall form; then, as we did with the eyebrows, strands can be defined.

Digitizing and Hair

Digitizing models that have sculpted hair tend to look like they're wearing helmets. If you want your model to look more natural, you might try leaving the hair off the digitizing model and using computer-generated hair instead.

> **TIP**
>
> **MAKING MOLDS FOR HAIR**
>
> Hair that lies along the surfaces of the scalp in braids and such can be applied individually to the head by sculpting the first braid, making many copies with a mold, and then applying them as you wish over the head. This method is from Richard Creager.
>
> 1. Using small rolled strands of Super Sculpey, form a braid long enough for your purpose.
> 2. Bake the braid and powder it with talc after it has cooled.
> 3. Push the braid into a small block of unbaked Super Sculpey.
> 4. Remove it carefully and bake the mold.
> 5. Apply talc to the braid mold after it has cooled and push more unbaked Super Sculpey into the mold. Remove the new braid.
> 6. Repeat, applying Super Sculpey in the mold for as many braids as you need.
>
> This technique also works well for adding scales on aliens.

Skin Texture

Using our tool to produce the fine wrinkles in the head was easy enough to do; however, if you're making a 3-foot-high animal, this could be a very time-consuming proposition. For these instances, there are easier ways to achieve the look of skin texture.

They say that necessity is the mother of invention. In this case, it's certainly true. Crumpled plastic wrap, orange peels—anything that will leave a mark—can be used for texturing skin. The only rule is, don't tile it so it looks like a pattern. Apply your texture just as nature does: randomly.

Some sculptors even make their own stamps to create scales and other designs for the skin. Tubing can be used to form rounded scales; however, the uniformity of it will tend to make the creature's skin look fake. If you will be using tubing, use different sizes to produce a non-uniform look.

After you have sculpted the head to your satisfaction, the head will remain in the same state until you bake it. It won't dry out or become hard to work with. If you want to set your piece up on a shelf for a few hours or even days to make sure you've captured the look you want, that's no problem. Many times after sculpting on a piece for many hours, I think, "Wow, that looks great," only to go back a few hours later and discover that the head doesn't look as good as I thought. (Hmmm, I must have been in denial.) Super Sculpey is a very forgiving clay—it will allow you the time to fix or change anything you want, right up to the moment it goes into the oven.

Now it's time to bake our creation.

Baking the Clay

Before the clay head can be baked, it's very important that you smooth the surfaces carefully with a brush and either saliva or acetone. Any unevenness left on the clay surface will be amplified when baked. This is especially important for areas like teeth and eyes. If you will be painting these surfaces, any bumpiness will be immediately noticeable and very hard to cover evenly with paint.

After the head has been smoothed to your satisfaction, any extra clay that is below the neckline on the wooden dowel must be removed. It's much simpler to remove it now, before it's baked, than to try to cut it off afterward. Don't worry about the length of the wooden dowel; it will be cut to length after the head has baked.

Now the head can be baked in the oven to harden.

1. Preheat your oven to 250 to 275 degrees. It's important for accurate timing that the oven already be at this temperature when the clay is placed in the oven.

2. Place the head on the sculpting stand in the middle of the oven.

3. Bake the clay for 20 minutes.

4. When the clay has baked, turn the oven off and leave the oven door open slightly. Do not take the head out of the oven.

5. Let the head cool in the oven for 30 to 40 minutes before taking it out.

Jodi Creager suggests wrapping the head in a towel to keep it warm as it cools down instead of leaving it in the oven. (Just make sure everyone knows it's there!) Any cracking usually occurs during the cooling-down process.

If the head looks like it's starting to crack, you may wind a rubber band around its width and length (from the chin to the top of the head) to hold it in place as it cools. If your head cracks anyway, you can fix it easily, as we'll see in the next section.

Fixing That Crack

Super Sculpey, as I've said before, is very forgiving. Almost anything can be fixed or repaired. You can even decide after the head has been baked that you really want a different-looking nose. It's no problem; just cut off the old nose and build a new one. The clay can be rebaked several times without harming the sculpture.

Super Sculpey is less forgiving, however, when it comes to cracks. Cracks appear in Super Sculpey sculptures for many reasons, most commonly:

- Baking at too high a temperature. Always use an oven thermometer to accurately set your oven's temperature.
- Air bubbles caught in the clay. This is typically from overkneading the clay or not forcing out air bubbles when applying more clay to the sculpture.

If cracks appear on your sculpture, follow these steps to repair them:

1. If the crack is large enough that pressing the head together closes the crack, run a bead of a super-strength glue down the crack as you hold it together. Be careful how you use super, or instant, glue on Super Sculpey; it will leave a shine on the surface and it can bond your fingers right to the head.

2. Add a thin layer of Super Sculpey over the crack and smooth the edges into the baked surface.

3. Smooth the edges with a brush and either saliva or acetone to make sure any seams will be invisible.

4. Making sure the oven is preheated, rebake head in the oven at 250 to 275 degrees for 10 minutes.

Using a Hair Dryer to Bake

Many times I have been in a situation in which a crack has appeared on one of my sculptures when I'm away from my oven, or the piece has been completed and I don't want to disassemble it to mend the crack. When this happens, I use my hair dryer as an alternative to an oven. To do this, fix the crack as described earlier. Then hold the hair dryer so it blows on the mended part on high heat until the repair hardens, about 10 minutes.

Now that the head had been baked, we'll smooth the surface again.

Surface Preparation After Baking

So, you smoothed your heart out before you baked and still the surface seems rough. That's typical of Super Sculpey. Here's an easy method if your sculpture still needs some polishing:

1. Using wet-dry sandpaper (600 grit), sand the surface of your creation under running water with Lava soap.

2. Rinse the sandpaper often to remove the clay from the grit.

This is especially useful for large, smooth areas like arms, legs, bodies, and so on. The surface will come out like porcelain.

Carving Super Sculpey

Super Sculpey can be sanded, drilled, sawed, and carved after it's baked. This allows you to add some unusual surface treatments or replace those you are disappointed with.

Now the head is ready to be attached to the body.

TIP

BURNISHING THE SURFACE

Using a smooth, polished rock is another effective way to smooth the large areas of the head other than teeth and eyes. When using rocks to smooth surfaces, be sure to use the right size to get into those hard-to-reach areas around the eyes. I usually have several polished stones available to switch to for different areas.

1. Place the unbaked head in the freezer. Leave for 15 minutes. The freezer will allow droplets of moisture to form on the surface of the oil-based clay.

2. Remove the head from the freezer, and using a smooth, polished rock, rub the surface of the clay in a circular manner.

Keep in mind that if you want to redo a portion of the head, with this method, you must do it all again, because when the head is placed back into the freezer, all burnishing done previously will disappear. Instead, you might consider using plain saliva and a polished rock to burnish, and skip the freezer technique. (See the Creager interview in Chapter 3.)

In Conclusion

The neck and shoulder anatomy is important for the right look of the head. It must be appropriate for the size and shape of the character. Now that this part is complete, we'll attach the head to the body..

In the Next Chapter

In Chapter 6, we'll use the simple wire armature from Chapter 2 to attach the head to the body and sculpt the body mass for the creature. We'll also add some detail to the body and discuss clothing, scales, and so on.

Chapter 6
Sculpting the Body

Chapter Objectives

- Learn body basics.
- Learn to sculpt hands.
- Learn to sculpt the body.
- Learn to add texture to the skin surface.
- Learn to bake the body.
- Learn to add sculpted hair.
- Learn to add clothing.
- Learn to paint the character.

Body Basics

In Chapter 5, we finished sculpting and firing the character's head. Now it's time to sculpt the body and attach the baked head. Using this system of creating parts separately and then combining them to form the character gives you some flexibility in design as well as letting you handle the fired pieces without worry that they will be accidentally deformed as you work.

In this chapter we start with a simple bent-wire armature, shown in Chapter 2, to match the character's size and position. We then sculpt the body structure to give the character its mass and shape.

To make the body armature, review Chapter 2 and follow the steps outlined in the section titled *Creating a Bent-Wire Armature.* Make sure to lay the wire over your drawn-to-scale schematic drawings so the size and shape of the skeleton will match your character's dimensions.

When the wire armature is bent into the appropriate shape, the character's hands can be addressed.

Hands

Hands are significant parts of the character's body, yet difficult to sculpt. Next to the head, expressive hands can tell much about the character's life and personality. Whether your character has aged, gnarled, arthritic hands or beautiful, delicate hands with long lovely nails, your audience will be able to tell something about the character just by looking at the hands. See Figure 6-1.

Figure 6-1 *The hands help tell the story of the character, as in this scene created by Richard and Jodi Creager.*

Stiff, straight hands on arms that hang limp might be good for that "dead" look, but if you want your character to be interesting to the viewer, a more exciting and lifelike pose is usually preferred.

Depending on the character you have designed, hands don't necessarily have to be human in form. Your character might have paws or claws, five fingers, three fingers, or none at all. In any case, knowing the form and function of human hands will provide you a reference point to work from to create any type of hand.

No matter what type of hands your character has, they are always of great interest to viewers. This fascination makes our work a little harder. People can't stop themselves from touching and "just bending them a bit." Delicate fingers break easily unless there is some type of base under the clay. For this reason, I use hand armatures to give my creatures' hands a better chance of surviving admirers.

The hand armature you'll create here is a basic human hand. This will give you a good understanding of how any character's hands can be created.

Hand Armatures

The hand armature is used primarily for characters with fingers or claws that protrude out from the body.

To begin, let's look at some rule-of-thumb measurements that are used when creating a basic human hand armature.

Hand Measurements

- The hand length from the base of the palm to the longest point of the middle finger is approximately the same as the distance from the character's chin to the midpoint of the forehead. The width is approximately half a head wide.

- From a top view, the shape of the hand, not including the thumb, approximates a rectangle. Notice that the lines running down both sides of the hand, along the outer edge of the fingers and palm, are straight.

- The length of the fingers at the longest point is approximately equal to the length of the palm. The fingers taper toward the end.

- From a side view the hand forms a wedge shape, having more thickness at the wrist and tapering down toward the fingers. Also, the inner edge of the hand (where the thumb is located) is thicker than the outer edge.

- Looking at the palm, you'll see that the fingers are attached to the palm in an arched line.

- The back of the hand lies in a straight plane with the arm.

- The thumb moves on a different plane from the rest of the fingers. Notice the thumb's length in reference to the first finger. The tip of the thumb falls between the first and second joint of the index finger.

- Each finger has three segments. The thumb has two.

These measurements will give you a good idea of the size and shape the hand should be. To get a better idea of how each part of the hand looks and works, let's look at some basic hand anatomy.

Hand Anatomy

There are 27 bones in a human hand and wrist. In the wrist there are eight irregularly shaped bones called the carpal bones. The palm of the hand is made up of five long, slender bones with rounded ends, called metacarpals. Last, but not least, are the fingers and thumb, made up of 14 short bones with the ends squared off, called phalanges.

The Carpal Bones

The carpal bones are clustered in the wrist and fit like a jigsaw puzzle with themselves as well as with the metacarpals and the bones of the forearm. The joint with the most mobility is at the base of the thumb. This includes the first metacarpal and the navicular bone in the wrist. There is also some mobility at the base of the fifth metacarpal (the smallest finger) and the hamate bone in the wrist. The rest of the wrist bones have little or no movement with the hand bones.

The Metacarpal Bones

The metacarpal bones make up the palm area of the hand. The four metacarpals directly under the four fingers of the hand cannot be separated or moved from each other. Only the first metacarpal, under the thumb, can be moved separately.

The Phalanges

The phalanges make up the fingers. There are three bones in each finger and two in the thumb. Notice that the bones in the fingers get a little smaller and more tapered as they get closer to the fingertip. The shapes of these bones will influence the shape of the fingers.

The squared bones, or phalanges, in the fingers have no side-to-side movement—not on purpose anyway. However, the joints between the metacarpals in the palm and the first phalanx in the fingers do have some side-to-side movement over the rounded edges of the metacarpals.

The squared ends of the phalanges show as knuckles on the backs of the fingers when a fist is made. The ends of the metacarpals also show on the backs of the hand when a fist is made, but they form a more rounded surface than the knuckles on the fingers.

Remember: There are no straight lines on the body. Every part of the body has some curve or arch to it. This is illustrated in Figure 6-2.

Figure 6-2 *This is the famous drawing of a woman's hands by Leonardo da Vinci. Look at the supple curves and shape of the hands.*

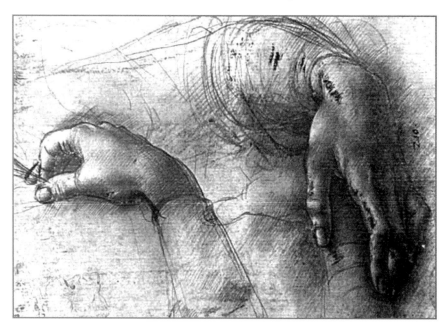

Make a fist and study your hand. Notice that the metacarpal joints are not in a straight line, but form an arch across the back of the hand. Notice also that the first two joints of the first and second fingers are more apparent, and the third and fourth joints appear to flatten out. (On fleshier hands, they might disappear altogether or form dimples where the joints are.)

The first knuckle usually sticks out further than the rest, followed by the second knuckle and so on. This is because the fat pad under the thumb is pulled in and gets in the way. When the fist is clenched, the skin on the back of the hands smooths out and the veins and tendons are compressed.

There are webs in between the fingers that separate the fingers and are slightly squared. The web between the thumb and the first finger is the most noticeable and allows the thumb greater mobility.

Remember the hand's shape when you sculpt. Look at your own hand and see, once again, that there are no straight lines. The hand from the side can be seen most simply as a tapered trapezoid. The outer edge of the hand is thinner than the thumb side. If you lay your hand flat and stick out your thumb, you see that the thumb starts almost at the base of the palm. Put your thumb alongside the rest of your fingers and you can see that the thumbnail sets on a different plane from as the rest of your fingernails. This is because the thumb's metacarpal bone (or the first metacarpal) is attached to the wrist on a plane nearly perpendicular to the other metacarpals in the hand. As you hold your hand on its side with it resting on the outside edge, you can hold the thumb out creating an L shape and see that in this position, the thumb first lies on a different plane than the rest of the fingers. Notice the thumb bends at a different angle from the other four fingers as well.

Lay your hand flat and look at the tapered fingers. The middle, or third, finger seems to be longer than the rest. One of the reasons for this is that it has longer phalanges, but it is also set higher on the palm than the other fingers. The line on the inside palm that runs at the base of the fingers is a curve. The first and fourth fingers are relatively the same size, but are shorter than the middle finger by nearly half a segment. The smallest finger, or fifth finger, is shorter than the fourth finger by a full segment.

Straighten your hand again and lay the fingers side by side. You'll see that the fingers lie snugly against one another because the knuckles are staggered. This occurs because of the curve of the palm and the different lengths of the fingers.

The middle finger is not only the longest but also the straightest and largest of the fingers. The other fingers taper toward it, making the hand more oval in shape and less like a box. The fingers also bend slightly toward the palm. Try to hold your fingers out straight; it is uncomfortable to try to hold that position for long.

There are four major fleshy pads in the palm. The first is the one at the base of the thumb. This ball-shaped pad is the most powerful part of the thumb. Next are the little pads that lie at the bases of the fingers. The last two pads are inside the palm and heel of the palm at the wrist, below the fourth and fifth fingers. These last two are the flattest, and when the hand comes together by touching the thumb to your fingers on one hand, the other two mostly obscure these pads.

The lines on the palm do more than make it amusing to go to a palm reader: They allow your hand to bend naturally. Look at your own hand, and bend your fingers to open and close. The fat pads contract, bunch up, and fold over onto themselves when the hand is opened and closed. Notice the lines of the palm in Figure 6-3.

Figure 6-3 *The open hand of this character created by Richard and Jodi Creager shows the palm lines distinctly.*

Creating the Hand Armature

Now that you have a better idea about how the hand looks and works, let's create the hand armature.

The armature is produced with 20-gauge floral wire and needle-nose pliers. The wire is thin enough to bend easily but strong enough to give some support so delicate fingers don't break off and destroy that "five fingers and five toes" look. My wire armatures are created in two parts, as discussed in Chapter 2. Review Chapter 2 to complete the wire armature.

Note: It is useful to draw the character's hands to scale, so you can simply lay the wire down over the drawing and mold it to the correct size and shape.

Once the basic hand armature has been created, give it a covering of aluminum foil to let the clay better adhere to the frame.

Because the hand is a delicate part of the anatomy, keep the thickness of the foil covering to a minimum. Otherwise, the fingers become overly bulky when clay is added. The foil is held onto the armature wire with hot-melt glue. Be careful not to put too much glue on, or you'll have lumps under the foil. To make sure there is only a single layer of foil on your fingers:

1. Cover each finger individually with a strip of foil the width of the wire finger circumference and long enough to cover the length of the finger and palm.

    Note: A good demonstration of this technique can be seen in Richard and Jodi Creager's video, "Sculpting the Hands." More information on this video can be found in the Appendix.

2. Add a small amount of hot-melt glue on the wire finger and apply the foil, being careful to squeeze it down tightly against the wire.

3. Once the fingers have been covered, cut a piece of foil large enough to wrap around the palm and back of the hand once, as shown in Figure 6-4.

Figure 6-4 *The aluminum foil has been applied to the entire hand.*

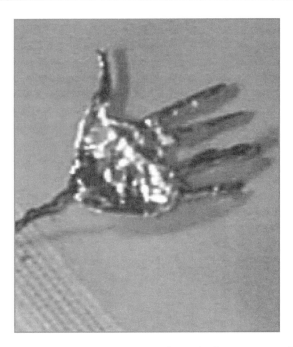

Now the hand is ready to be bent into its final position before clay is added. This is a very important step, as the wire fingers will not move after clay has been applied without deforming the clay.

Positioning the Wire Hand Armature

The hand is most comfortable when bent slightly toward the palm. Notice that when the wire hand is bent forward, the loops of the wire between the fingers at the palm come out to produce the knuckles on the backs of the hand, as shown in Figures 6-5a and b. This will give you a reference point to work from when you're sculpting hand details.

Figure 6-5a *The bare wire hand armature is bent toward the palm to allow the loops between the fingers to protrude and form the knuckles.*

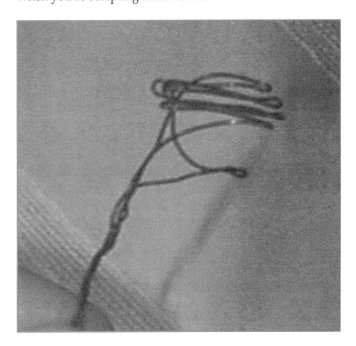

Figure 6-5b *The hand armature has a foil covering and has been bent into position.*

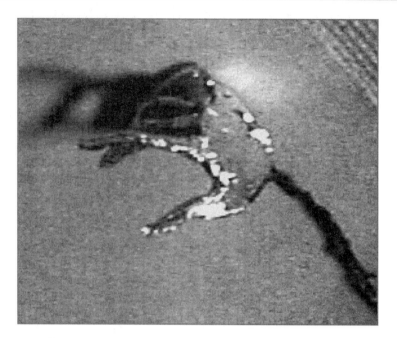

To create a more realistic-looking hand, keep the following tips in mind:

- The finger joints must be bent at sharp angles. Remember, the bones in the hands are solid and bend only at the joints. Therefore, a rounded bend at the joints won't provide a realistic look for the fingers.

- If your character will be holding an object, you must have the object prior to sculpting the hands. The object must be placed in the hand at the time the fingers are positioned for sculpting. This makes it easier to position the hand accurately.

- If possible, the object to be held should be baked in the hand to provide assurance that it will stay in the hand after the character is finished. If the object must be removed, make sure there is support to allow the hand to hold it easily.

- To create a small character holding a large and heavy object, the object must have some support of its own. That means a wire protruding from the object that goes into the base, or having the object resting on the base rather than the character holding the heavy object in mid-air.

Adding Clay to the Hands

After the hand armature has been posed, it's time to add clay. The most important part of this process is to make sure the wire is completely covered and you've given yourself enough clay on the surface to add details.

It doesn't really matter how you add the clay to the hand. Some people like to start with small pieces of clay and add to each section of the hand, while others take a single pancake of clay, wrap it around the hand, and then sculpt in details. I like to work in small pieces, on one side of the hand at a time. This gives me a little more control over how much clay I have in any given area.

1. Create flattened worms of clay the length of the fingers and apply to the back side of each finger, wrapping the clay around to cover the wire armature as shown in Figure 6-6. Remember that this is just a base for the hand. You'll add more clay to the areas that need it as you go along.

Figure 6-6 *The worms of clay are applied to the fingers.*

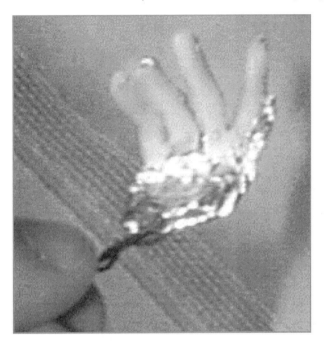

2. Flatten out a ball of clay approximately $1/8$ inch thick. Apply it to the palm of the wire hand.

3. Add small balls of clay to form the fat pads of the palm, as shown in Figure 6-7. Look at your own hands for reference.

Figure 6-7 *A small bail of clay is flattened for palm of the hand.*

4. Add the palm lines as shown in Figure 6-8. Make sure to bring the lines out to the sides of the hand as well. These are the creases that allow the hands to move and give more realism to the hand.

Figure 6-8 *The creases in the palm allow the hand to bend.*

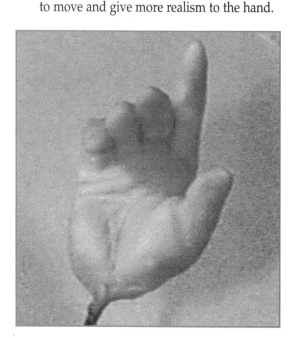

5. Add the web of skin that joins the thumb to the first finger.
6. Add more clay to each finger to give the right shape. Remember, the fingers are tapered.

    Now you're ready to add joints to the fingers.

1. Still working on the palm side of the hand, mark the positions of the joint lines for each finger with your wooden tool, as shown. Make sure the creases go all the way to the sides of the fingers, as shown in Figure 6-9. Bend your fingers and look at the creases created.

Figure 6-9 *The crease lines for the joints can be seen on the sides of the fingers.*

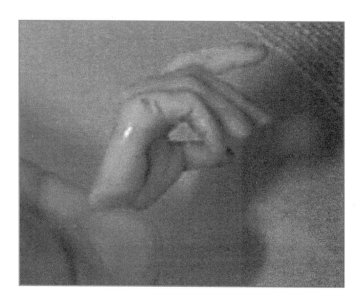

2. Turn the hand so you are looking at the back side. Lay the wooden tool flat on the back of the hand between each finger, angle the stick toward the center of the wrist, and make a slight indention in the clay as shown in Figure 6-10. This will give you a reference point as to where the hand ligaments are located. Remember that the younger your character is, the less noticeable the ligaments will be.

Figure 6-10 *The indentations on the back of the hand form a fan and show where the ligaments lie in the hand.*

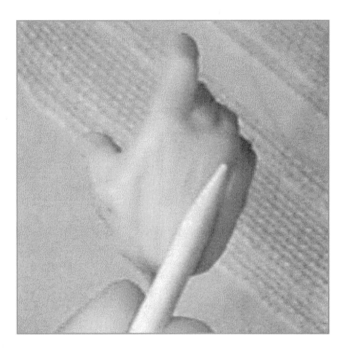

3. Make small holes on each finger to locate the knuckles at each joint.

4. Place tiny balls of clay on each hole and smooth the sides of the balls into the fingers, leaving the bulk of the added clay to form the knuckle, as shown in Figure 6-11. For more arthritic hands, the clay balls can be a little larger.

Figure 6-11 *The added clay has created knuckles on the fingers.*

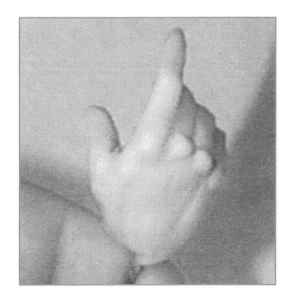

Adding Veins to the Hands

Veins can be added to the backs of the hands to give them a realistic touch.

1. Roll small bits of clay into tiny worms.
2. Lay the worms on the back of the hands to place the veins, as shown in Figure 6-12. Make sure the veins are lying on the hand in the opposite direction of the ligament lines.

Figure 6-12 *Small worms of clay are added to form veins on the backs of hands.*

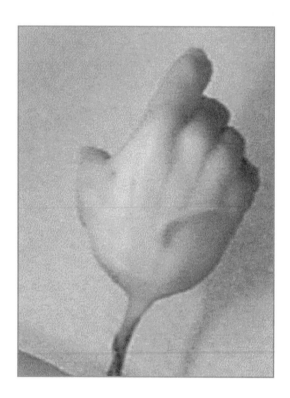

3. Press the worms slightly with the rounded side of the wooded stick, being careful not to roll away the detail.
4. Brush the veins with a small amount of acetone if necessary.

Adding Fingernails

Fingernails are easy to create with the wooden stick tool. They can be created out of Super Sculpey like the hand was, or out of other clays such as Cernit or Fimo. These clays come in a more translucent, white color and give a waxy, smooth surface for a "real nail" look. Using these other clays can be especially useful for characters with long nails or claws.

To sculpt basic nails on hands:

1. Press the flat side of the wooden sculpting tool into the nail bed area of the finger, as shown in Figure 6-13.

Figure 6-13 *The wooden tool is used to press a nail bed into the finger.*

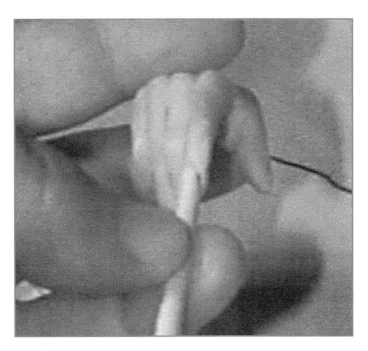

2. Using the edge of the tool, press into the sides of the finger to form the nail shape.

3. Bring the front edge of the nail up slightly from the finger with the tool, as shown in Figure 6-14.

4. Smooth the clay on the nail with a brush.

Figure 6-14 *The front edge of the nail bed is lifted with the wooden tool to create the front edge of the nail.*

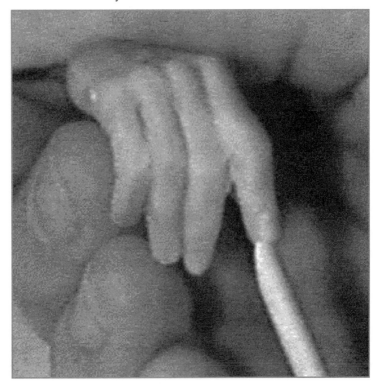

To add long nails:

Sometimes short nails just aren't right for your character. In this case, other clays such as Cernit can be used to form long ones.

1. Follow steps 1 through 3 for adding fingernails.
2. Using the flat end of the wooden tool, remove excess clay from the nailbed.
3. Using a small piece of Cernit clay, form a nail of the appropriate size and length.
4. Lay the Cernit nail onto the nail bed as shown in Figure 6-15.

Figure 6-15 *The Cernit nail is added to the clay finger.*

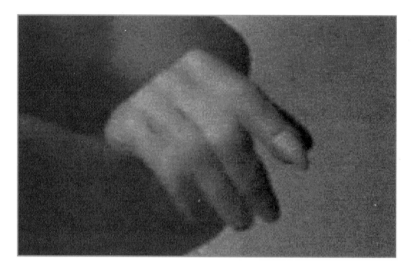

5. With the flat end of the wooden tool, press the new nail into the clay slightly, pressing around the edges to make the nail appear to be growing from the finger, not just layered on top. See Figure 6-16.

Figure 6-16 *The nail now looks as if it is part of the finger.*

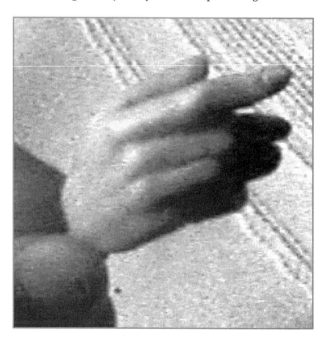

Tip: If the finger doesn't come up around the nail enough, use the stick to roll the clay around the edges of the nail.

To Add Claws

Claws can be problematic when applying them as long nails are applied. If they are too long, they tend to curl. To avoid this, make your claws and bake them first. Then apply them as you would apply long nails.

Baking the Hands

After the hands are sculpted, bake them with the wrist wire placed into a spare piece of clay to hold the hands up as they bake. If this isn't possible, lay the hands down carefully on crumpled paper towel in an ovenproof pan.

Bake at 275 degrees for 15 minutes.

When the hands are baked, they can be applied to the arm of the body armature by twisting the longer wrist wire that goes up the arm onto the heavier arm wire of the body armature. The wire can be attached with hot-melt glue before aluminum foil is applied.

Now that we have the hands ready, let's move on to the body.

The Body

The body of your character can actually be created in many ways. In this chapter we discuss sculpting the body in clay and building a simple body in cloth.

The Cloth Body

A simple cloth body can be very effective in creating characters, as it eliminates the excess body weight that results when you sculpt the body with clay. It is best to create the body before sculpting the neck and shoulderplate on your character. (See Chapter 5 for more information on shoulder plate creation.) Because the cloth will allow some flexibility, a cloth body can be dressed more easily, eliminating the need to "build an outfit" onto the character.

The best materials to use in the manufacture of the cloth body are fabrics that are strong yet flexible. Heavy muslin, canvas, and faux leather or suede materials are serviceable choices. The body you create can be as simple or as complex as your character demands. I use a simple pattern, shown in Figure 6-17.

How you decide to make your body is up to you. However, there are some simple rules to keep in mind:

Rule 1: Always stitch the pieces of the cloth body securely, or glue with a good fabric glue, to ensure strong seams when stuffing.

Rule 2: Place the cloth body skin over the armature before stuffing. This allows the armature wires to be correctly embedded in the stuffed body.

Rule 3: Always stuff the body as tightly as possible. After you've stuffed it until there is certainly no more space, put it down for a while and come back later to stuff it some more. You will usually find some way to get just a little more of that stuffing inside the body.

Figure 6-17 *A simple torso pattern can be used for male or female characters.*

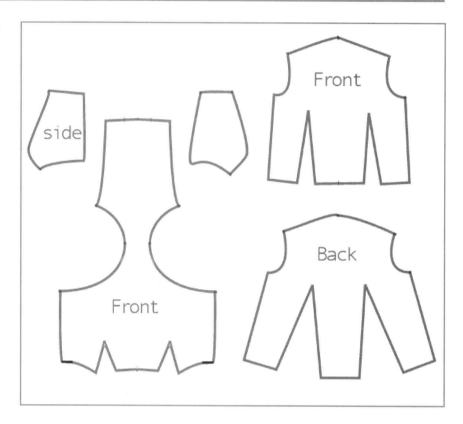

Adding Sculpted Arms and Legs

Adding sculpted arms and legs to characters with cloth bodies is a simple procedure. However, like everything else, you must plan ahead. How you will sculpt the arms and legs will depend on how your character will look. Will the character have muscular arms, bare to the shoulders? Or will a long-sleeved shirt cover the arms? This will determine how much of the arm or leg needs to be sculpted and how much can be cloth. Another thing to consider is what type of armature you will be using. If a simple bent-wire armature is the answer, you must build and bake the arms and legs onto the armature before the cloth body is added. This keeps fabrics that scorch, melt, or burn from being ruined while you bake the Sculpey arms and legs. If the armature comes apart like the one shown in Chapter 2, Figure 2-2, you can add the arms and legs after the body has been completed. Simply sculpt and bake arms and legs on the correct armature part, then add the body to the torso section of the armature. When the arms and legs have been fired, simply pop everything back together.

Here are the steps to attach sculpted arms and legs to cloth bodies:

1. With the wire armature as the base, add aluminum foil and clay in the correct locations on the wire to sculpt arms and legs.

2. After sculpting, a groove is created in the clay with the side of the wooden tool around the part's circumference, $1/8$ to $1/4$ inch below the top edge of the appendage, as shown in Figure 6-18. This is where the cloth portion will attach to the sculpted piece.

Figure 6-18 *A groove is created around the circumference ¹/₈ to ¹/₄ inch below the top edge of the limb so it can be attached to the cloth portion.*

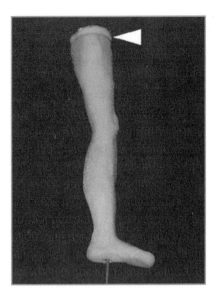

3. Bake at 250 degrees for 20 minutes. Allow to cool.

4. Cut out pattern pieces for upper legs and arms as shown in Figure 6-19, making sure they are long enough to go completely around the sculpted part and wide enough to cover the area from the top of the sculpted part to the cloth body. Be sure to leave a minimum ¹/₈ inch allowances for seams.

Figure 6-19 *Pattern pieces for upper arms and legs.*

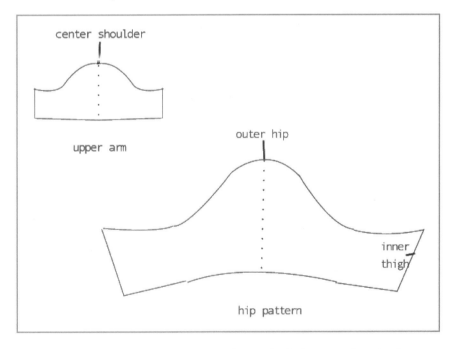

5. With right sides together, sew or glue each cloth piece along back seam. Wait for glue to dry if you've used fabric glue.

6. Slide cloth part (still inside out) over matching sculpted part with the bottom edge of the cloth lying along the top edge of the sculpted part, as shown in Figure 6-20.

Figure 6-20 *The top edge of the upper cloth leg is lying along the top edge of the sculpted leg.*

7. Run a bead of glue along the indentation at the upper edge of the sculpted part.

8. Press the cloth into position, wrap floral wire around the leg inside the groove, and twist.

9. Bring the cloth back up over the top of the sculptured leg, forming the upper part as shown in Figure 6-21.

10. Now you're ready to stuff and sew the legs and arms onto the body.

Figure 6-21 *The cloth is brought back up over the leg to create the upper portion.*

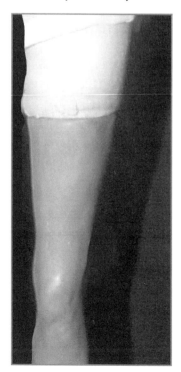

Sculpting Bodies

Sculpting bodies can be easier in some ways than building them in cloth. There's no pattern, no sewing, just working with the clay. Arms and legs can be sculpted at the same time the body is sculpted so that you don't have to worry about things not matching up. However, before you can start sculpting the body mass, you must understand how your character's body is designed. Review basic body structure in Chapter 2. Look at books on anatomy and physiology to visualize how the muscles lie on the body surface and how they change shape with body movement. Good reference books such as *Atlas of Human Anatomy for the Artist* by Stephen Rogers Peck, *Drawing the Head and Figure* by Jack Hamm, and *Anatomy for the Artist* by Jeno Barcsay are invaluable to the sculptor.

There are differences in bodies just as there are differences in facial features. The race, age, and sex of your character will affect the design. The male and female bodies are alike in most gross aspects; that is, both have two arms, two legs, and so on. The primary areas of difference are alignment and mass. There are other minor differences in skeletal areas such as the pelvis. As a rule, the female is smaller overall than the male, except at the hips. Her body has more fat covering the skeleton; thus, her body is less angular and more rounded.

In the neck and shoulder area, the female appears more slender and graceful than the male. This is caused by the shape and size of the shoulders. They are smaller in the female, and the clavicles (or collarbones) tend to angle downward toward the sternum (or breastbone), making the shoulders look more rounded. In the male, the clavicles tend to be straighter, making the shoulders wider. A male has a more squared look than a female.

The torso of the female is somewhat longer than that of the male in relation to total body height. The chest is shorter and rounder on a female and shows the female breast development. The female pelvis is shorter but wider and deeper, and it tilts forward slightly to facilitate childbirth. This makes the female spinal lumbar curve a slightly deeper arch.

The female also usually has shorter arms and legs than the male. Be sure to take this into account if you attempt to change a male character to a female or vice versa. Most of the height differences between females and males can be found in the upper arm (the humerus) and along the entire leg. Normally, the upper arm is shorter on a female anyway, placing her elbow a little higher than his. Her wrists and hands are also smaller.

The female thigh is shorter than the male's because of the femur's greater angle coming from the female's wider pelvis. This causes the more curved look of the female hips as they come down toward the knees.

Be sure to note that the lower leg is also a little shorter in the female than in the male. Because of distributed fat, the female leg tends to be smoother, and the swelling of the calf is also slightly lower on her leg. The female ankle is rounder and less prominent than that of the male, and her feet are smaller and narrower.

While differences between the sexes can be seen in the skeleton, the most striking differences can be seen in the layer of body fat. The female body carries more fat than the male and every area of the body is affected. It is what makes the female body round and voluptuous.

Body Muscles

Whatever sex your character is, muscle mass will determine the basic shape of the body. Muscles encapsulate the bones of the body you're creating, and give the body's form dimension and shape. There are four body types to remember.

The Average Type

This type has a pretty even distribution of fat, giving a sleek appearance. There is a good proportion of muscle; however, it is not overly defined or angular as in the muscular type.

The Muscular Type

This is the Arnold Schwarzenegger of body types. It is an exaggeration of normal musculature. Some of the features of this type are larger upper body, large thighs, large neck, and excessive muscle definition in the back. Usually this body type cannot lay its arms down to the side because of bulging muscles. Remember that this type will not be able to stand or move the same way as the average type. Compensation will have to be made for the bulging muscles.

The Obese Type

Has your model been hiding food in the chandelier again? This type should have him covered. Just as the muscular type was an exaggeration of normal, so is the obese type an exaggeration of normal in body fat. It is characterized by a round, voluminous shape. The body weight is centered in the abdomen and the tissue jiggles with movement. Rolls of fat are apparent around neck and legs, keeping those thighs from coming together. Fat in the chest, torso area, and arms also keeps arms from coming down to the sides. Usually wrists and ankles are near normal size. However, they can be heavy as well due to disease or water retention.

The Very Thin Type

This is the Ally McBeal of body types. Characterized by a frail appearance, it lacks most fat and muscle, leaving only a thinly covered skeletal figure. The thighs don't come together at the crotch. The joints look overly large, as well as the pelvis. The ribs and breastbone are very noticeable on this type.

Knowing these body types will help you choose the right one for the personality of your character. But whichever you choose, some basic body structure remains the same when sculpting.

Remember that the arms and legs aren't just stuck to the torso. They are connected with bone, cartilage, and muscle, and everything always moves together.

Fleshing Out the Body Armature

Once your armature is created and you have a basic structure designed, start adding a core of aluminum foil, following the shape needed for your character. This will give the necessary bulk to the body shape without adding the weight of extra clay.

WHEN SCULPTING THE BODY

Look at the body diagram in Figure 6-22.

There are several things to keep in mind when you sculpt a body.

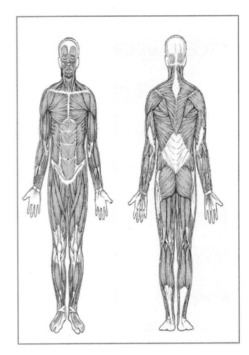

Figure 6-22 *The body muscles front and back.*

Upper Body

- When sculpting the upper arm, notice that it always appears to "tuck under" the chest muscles from any angle. In a relaxed position with arms down to the side, the arm lies against the torso and the lower arm angles slightly forward from the elbow. When an arm is raised, the muscles from the armpit and chest seem to be woven together and the top line of the shoulder changes as the shoulder, clavicle, scapula, and torso move along with the arm. With the arm raised completely over the head, the midpoint between the finger-tips and the floor is the figure's navel.

- The figure's total height from the top of the head to the floor is the same as the distance between right and left hand fingertips when arms are stretched out to the side.

- Remember that the arms lie next to the torso when brought down to the side. If there is a large gap between arms and chest, either the arms or the chest lacks the proper muscle mass.

- In a muscular, fit body, the sides of the chest angle up toward the shoulder from the waist, and the stomach and lower chest muscles are clearly defined.

- As the arms are raised, the armpit goes up and in toward the shoulder.

- There is a visible definition of the pectoral muscles in the chest, showing a slight indentation between them running along the breastbone.

- In a female figure, the breasts are usually located between the third and sixth ribs. They are hemispherical in shape and the base of the breast is connected to the chest by skin extending back along the pectoral muscles to the armpit.

- The bottom of the ribcage is usually defined, unless the character is obese.

Lower Body

- Notice that the legs aren't just straight cylinders, but are staggered. The thigh is offset to the outside and in front of the lower leg.

- The legs taper down to the ankles.

- The distance from the shoulder to the elbow is equal to the distance from the bottom of the buttocks to the knee.

- The distance from the elbow to the fingertips is equal to the distance between the knee and the heel.

- Notice the curvature of the leg: The inside curve differs from the outside curve.

The foil is applied to the wire armature with hot-melt glue and must be tightly compact on the wire, as shown in Figures 6-23 (top).

Figure 6-23 *Top: Aluminum foil has been added to the armature of this character to produce lightweight bulk. Bottom: The finished cat created by Cynthia Cox, student at The Art Institute of Phoenix.*

Be careful to add only enough foil to create the core of the body. Leave room for an additional layer of clay at least $1/4$ inch thick. A $1/4$-inch layer of clay won't crack easily, and has enough depth to add musculature and detail.

1. Tear pieces of aluminum foil approximately 10 inches square.

2. Using a hot-glue gun, add melted hot glue to the armature spine. This will keep the foil from sliding on the armature.

3. Wrap foil over the hot glue on the spine and press tightly to make sure the foil is tight.

   Tip: Tightly pressed pads of foil can be glued over areas where more bulk is required, such as breasts, buttocks, or large bellies. The pads are glued into place with hot-melt glue and then covered with an additional layer of foil to smooth out transitions between surfaces.

4. Continue adding glue and foil to the body, remembering to leave the wire bare that will come out the bottom of the character's feet into the stand.

Figure 6-24 *This character, created by Dana Vitucci, student at The Art Institute of Phoenix, was sculpted in the shape of its clothes.*

Note: Make sure any extra wires on the armature that have been applied for significantly protruding parts, such as large ears, tails, horns, or spikes, are covered with a layer of foil as well.

Attaching the Head to the Body

Before the head can be attached, it must be baked. (See Chapter 5.) The wooden dowel protruding from the neck must then be cut even with the base of the neck, and a hole must be drilled into the remaining piece of wooden dowel to take the neck wire of the body armature.

1. Using an appropriate type of saw (a razor saw works well for this), saw off the wood dowel flat at the base of the neck. Make sure to hold onto the head carefully as you saw, to prevent cracking or breaking the baked clay.

2. Using a $1/8$-inch drill bit in an electric drill, slowly drill a hole up from the bottom of the wood dowel into the head. The penny will stop the drill from going too far.

3. Measure the drilled hole in the wood dowel by sliding the neck wire into the hole. This will determine the length of the neck wire needed on the body armature.

4. Cut the body armature neck wire to match the length of the drilled hole in the wooden dowel.

5. The head can now be placed onto the neck wire. The head and neck should sit directly on top of the shoulders.

Now the body is ready for clay.

> **TIP**
>
> ## CHARACTERS WITH LARGE HEADS AND SMALL BODIES
>
> If your character has an extremely large head and a very small body, the figure will be top-heavy. Keep the following tips in mind;
>
> - Set the armature leg wires in a heavy wooden block base that has been drilled to accept the wires. This will keep the character from falling on its face.
>
> - Build up the mass of the body with clay before the head is attached to the armature. This allows the weight of the body to have some counterbalance effect.
>
> - Make sure the character's weight is centered over the feet. The larger the feet are, the more stable the character will be.

Sculpting the Body with Clothes

The shape of your character's body will depend on your final design. If your character has sculpted clothing, as in Figure 6-24, either the character's body is sculpted in the shape of the clothes, or layers of clay can be rolled and cut out like cloth and applied to the clay surface of the body.

Both methods give you great flexibility regarding the way the clothes lie and wrinkle on the surface. They also give you freedom to create small details on the surface, which is much harder to do with fabric. If you wish to try your hand at creating nonremovable clothing from cloth, leather, or fur, the character's body need only be sculpted in its basic body shape. Remember, if the character will appear with little or no clothing, the exposed body must be sculpted to match the appropriate anatomy.

When the head is attached to the foil-wrapped armature, start applying clay. One of the easiest ways to sculpt a body is in layers. Follow these steps for this method:

1. Apply clay in the shoulder area, smoothing the clay up into the baked clay neck of the character, as shown in Figure 6.25.

2. Smooth the new clay with acetone and a brush where it comes in contact with the baked clay, so no visible seams or patches appear.

    Note: The clay must provide a continuous skin between the body and the head so that when the finished piece is baked, the head and body will be one.

3. Sculpt the basic body mass without fine details such as folds and wrinkles, veins, and so on.

4. Smooth the clay, making sure all unwanted lumps and uneven surfaces have been removed.

Figure 6.25 *Alvaro Chavez, a student at The Art Institute of Phoenix, has smoothed the clay on his sculpture from the shoulders up into the head to make one continuous skin.*

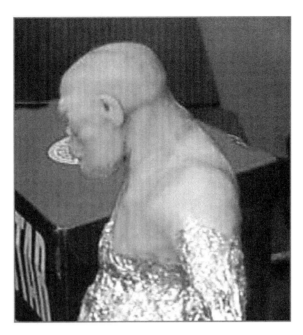

5. Bake the body. (See "Baking the Body" later in this chapter for more information on baking the clay.)

6. After the baked clay has cooled, a second layer of clay can be applied to the body to sculpt in all the fine details.

7. Smooth the clay and brush the areas where the two clays come together with acetone to eliminate any seams that might show up on the finished sculpture.

Sculpting Feet

Sculpting feet on characters is one of the easier tasks. The foot is always sculpted in its final form. In other words, if the character is wearing shoes, the foot is sculpted in the shape of the shoe. However, if the character's feet are exposed, the entire exposed portion will be sculpted to match the anatomy of the character, as shown in Figure 6-26.

Since most characters are standing on their feet, there's seldom a problem with breakage; therefore, I usually don't require a foot armature as I do with the hands. However, in some instances it may be essential for your character's feet to have a wire base. This is recommended when the feet are raised in the air in an action pose, or if the character has huge toes or claws rising up from the foot, leaving it vulnerable to chips and dings. In most cases, the wire leg armature simply passes through the sculpted foot and into a wooden stand, leaving the sculpted foot resting on the wooden surface to give it support.

If the raised foot needs extra support, the armature leg wire that would ordinarily pass through the foot into the stand can be bent in a U shape the size of the foot, and foil can be applied to give it support. Since the foot will not be attached to the ground, an armature wire protruding through the foot is unnecessary. Remember that this puts all the character's weight on the opposite foot,

Figure 6-26 *Sculpting all the foot anatomy is only necessary when the feet are bare.*

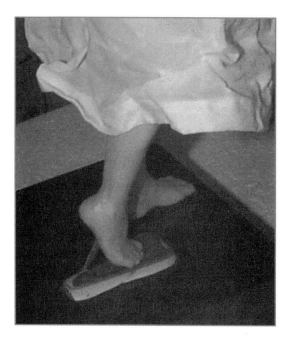

so make sure the supporting foot wire is long and heavy enough to hold the character.

Note: If you prefer, bending the foot wires of your character into position and strapping them onto a baked piece of Super Sculpey or wood for support will also keep your character in place.

Methods of Texturing Skin

1. Create stamps of texture or scales out of Super Sculpey that has been baked and is then used to press a pattern into the soft Super Sculpey skin. Be careful to change the angle and placement of the stamp to avoid a "wallpaper" effect.

2. Use organic and household items as stamps. Crumpled up plastic wrap or orange peel gives a nice effect.

3. X-acto knives and wire tools allow you to "carve" texture into the surface before baking.

4. X-acto knives can also be used to carve the Super Sculpey surface after it's been baked.

Veins

1. Roll a small worm of clay with your finger on a flat surface until the worm is very thin.

2. Place the worm of clay on the surface where you want a vein to protrude from the skin.

3. Hold one end of the worm and pull slightly to break the worm at the appropriate length. This gives a tapered end to the worm.

4. Use a brush with acetone to smooth the vein into the skin, making sure not to smooth it too much.

TIP

ADDING TEXTURE IN CLAY

If your character needs sculpted skin texture, scales, feathers, veins, and so on, as in Figure 6-27, you can apply the texture to the clay before it is baked, or apply it to the detail layer.

Figure 6-27 *Katharine Hargroves, student at The Art Institute of Phoenix, has made several character sculptures requiring skin textures of different types.*

Baking the Body

After the body sculpting has been completed, it is time for the final baking process. If your character is small, you should have no problem simply standing the character on its wooden stand in the oven. Unfortunately, this is seldom the case. (See Figure 6-28.)

Most characters will need to lie horizontally to fit into an oven; in some cases, a custom oven will have to be built to accommodate the figure. If your character will fit into your oven lying horizontally, use crumpled paper towel in a flat pan to fire the character. This will help the clay from deforming while baking. Never use foil to bake the character on. It will cut into the clay.

Super Sculpey bakes at 275 degrees. If you bake the clay at too high a temperature, toxic gases can be emitted. If you are unsure about the accuracy of your oven's temperature, buy a cheap oven thermometer to make sure the clay is being baked at the correct temperature. Don't place parts of the sculpture too close to a heating element in the oven. This will scorch the clay.

Figure 6-28 *This figure is too large for a conventional oven. In a case like this, a makeshift oven can be devised.*

Most 18-inch clay figures will cook in approximately 20 minutes. However, if your sculpture has an unusually thick layer of clay, the time to bake the sculpture could be as long as 50 to 60 minutes. The clay will feel like hard rubber when it's first removed from the oven. It will harden more as it cools.

Cracking during Baking

Super Sculpey sometimes cracks as it is cooling from the baking process. This occurs when the oven temperature is too high, or when bubbles are left in the clay. Sometimes the clay cracks at pressure points when the clay is pressed in, as with the temple area of the head. These cracks are easily repaired. If you see that the sculpture is starting to crack, wrap a rubber band carefully around the part to hold it together until it's cooled. This works particularly well for the head.

When baking characters, keep the following rules in mind:

- There is a mild odor as the clay cooks. If the smell gets too strong or you see smoke, your clay is starting to burn. Remove from the oven immediately.

- When baking sculptures for the second time, cover thin areas of clay such as ears with foil.

- If you are unsure of the oven's thermostat, use an oven thermometer to check the accuracy of the oven's temperature.

A CUSTOM OUTDOOR OVEN

If a custom oven is needed, one can be constructed quite easily.

This particular oven was created by Shaun Cook, a student at The Art Institute of Phoenix. Remember, this is an outdoor oven. Do not use this indoors!!!

Supplies needed for oven:

One 2 – 3-foot piece of chicken or cage wire

1 box heavy-duty aluminum foil

A small wire rack (approximately 8 × 10 inches). (Either use the grill from a small barbecue, or create a rack from a double layer of the chicken or cage wire.)

A Charcoal Chimney or small charcoal grill (hibachi).

Charcoal briquettes

Duct tape

1 block of scrap wood with holes drilled large enough to hold the sculpture.

Instructions for oven construction:

1. Roll chicken or cage wire into a cylinder shape and hook wire ends onto themselves to hold shape. Note that the wire rack you use should be large enough to cover the cylinder opening at the bottom edge.

2. Cover wire cylinder with two layers of heavy-duty aluminum foil.

3. Seal edge with duct tape.

4. Cut a piece of aluminum foil large enough to fold in half and still cover the top of the cylinder.

5. Mold the edges of the aluminum foil over the cylinder to form a lid. The bottom of the cylinder will remain open.

6. Cover the wire rack and wood block with one layer of aluminum foil.

Cooking instructions:

1. Fill chimney or hibachi with charcoal.

2. Light the coals and let them burn down until all coals turn white and you can hold your hand close to the grill without burning yourself. **This can take some time; never place your hand any closer than is comfortable.**

3. Place the foil-covered wire rack over the coals. If you can *very briefly* place your hand on the rack, your coals are ready for the oven.

   Note: Don't let the coals get too cool, or you'll have to start over!

4. Place sculpture on wooden block, placing armature wire through the aluminum foil and into drilled holes so your sculpture is standing upright.

5. Place wooden block and sculpture in the center of the wire rack.

6. With a pencil or screwdriver, poke three or four holes into the aluminum foil on the wire rack, making sure not to place any holes directly under the wooden block or any other parts of the sculpture extending beyond the wooden block. These holes let heat into your oven. The more holes, the more heat. Remember, you only need the oven set to 275 degrees. *WARNING:* Never place your hand on the wire rack after holes have been created!!

7. Carefully set wire cylinder with lid over sculpture and hibachi. You can check the temperature of the oven by waiting 5 minutes. Then lay your hand on the cylinder's foil lid. It should be very warm, but not hot.

8. Depending on the temperature of your oven and the thickness of the clay, your character might take 30 to 40 minutes to cook, or even longer.

9. Check the sculpture after 20 minutes by carefully lifting the cylinder with oven mitts. Don't lift the lid to check the sculpture very often. Every time you lift the lid, your oven will lose heat.

10. Your sculpture is done when it feels hot to the touch and feels like hard rubber. It will harden more as it cools.

    Note: If you need to bake your character a second time, be sure to put new aluminum over the wire rack.

Surface Finishing on Baked Clay

Surface finishing is important, especially for characters that will be painted. A smooth finish allows the paint to be applied evenly and produces a professional-looking finished product. No matter how much smoothing you did before baking, afterward the surface is always somewhat rough. To smooth the baked surface, use 600-grit wet-dry sandpaper and Lava soap. Wet the sandpaper and apply the soap. Then sand the baked clay under running water.

Painting Skin Tones

Paint can be applied to your character after the clay has been baked to give your character a more lifelike appearance, as shown in Figure 6-29.

No skin color is a solid and flat. It is produced by dozens of colors, shades and tints. To produce more realistic skin tones on your character, colors must be layered on the surface to produce the desired effect and give the skin color depth. I paint the character's skin in layers so that each layer shows the colors beneath.

Note: As an extra bonus, painting the character can also be used to visualize texture maps and shadowing for a computer-generated character.

Figure 6-29 *This character, created by Donald Jenny, a student at The Art Institute of Phoenix, has skin texture applied with paint rather than by incising the clay.*

Paint Types

Super Sculpey can be painted with any kind of paint except enamels. If you use enamels on this clay, it will never dry. I prefer to use chalk pastels and acrylic; however, water colors and oil paint are also used.

Chalk Pastels

I prefer to use chalk pastels to cover the clay surface. The chalk is transparent enough to see all the layers of color clearly and the pastels give a soft look to the skin tone.

Here are a few tips for working with chalk pastels:

- Use Rembrandt brand pastels. They are smoother and creamier to work with. A bit more expensive, they can be bought by the piece to eliminate higher costs.

- Make two palettes with pastel art paper. Rub the colors onto the paper you will be using so you can pick the colors up off the palette with a brush to apply them to the clay. I use the first palette for lighter foundation skin tones. Depending on the color of the character's skin, a variety of skin-tone colors—beige, browns, roses, reds, peaches, and so on—and a small amount of light gray-blue and yellow are used. The second palette is for darker tones of browns and blacks. Your palettes will depend on your character.

- When using pastels, it is important to note that the chalk will not simply wipe off the clay. The oil base of the clay holds the chalk tightly to the surface. The chalk can be smoothed and diluted with water; however, it's a good idea to apply lighter colors first.

- A cut-down makeup brush or a short, stubby flat brush to apply the pastels is useful. The more you rub the color, the more paint gets down into the clay, resulting in a more even color.

- Brush over the entire surface to create the basic skin tones with your large, stubby brush. Then use a smaller brush to get into areas you can't reach with the larger one, such as around the eyes and nose.

- Brush rosy tones in the cheek area. Add gray-blue wherever the skin is thin: under the eyes, at the inside corners between the eyes, and at the nose and the temples. Also add gray wherever you want shadows. You can add some yellows around the mouth and nose. (Reference books are available on theatrical makeup that will give you more ideas about how to paint skin tones appropriate to your character.)

Water-Based Paint

Acrylics are used for painting hair, eyes, lips, under-skin veins, and age or beauty marks. They're also useful diluted as washes. Washes can be applied in layers for darker skin tones to give a more realistic look.

Acrylics used for veins and age spots are painted onto the clay before washes or chalks are used for skin tones. This gives the illusion that they are below the skin. An Eagle Prismacolor pencil can be used to draw veins on the surface; then rub them slightly with your finger to make them less obvious. You don't want big blue lines painted all over the surface of the skin (unless that's the look you want for your creature). The color I use is slate gray #936.

Water-based paints are somewhat more difficult to use than the pastels, because you are applying water to an oil surface. The paint tends to bead on the surface for the first couple of layers. Paper towels can be used to blot up the excess. After the first couple of layers dry, the clay will be sealed enough to eliminate this problem.

Airbrushing

Airbrushing can be a great way to paint your character if you have a light touch. It is necessary to mask off all areas you don't want painted, but it will give you a smooth, flawless finish.

Painting the Eyes

If you sculpted the eyes and want the sculpture to be a finished maquette rather than a digitizing model, you will need to paint the eyes to add realism. Painting allows you to focus the eyes in any direction after the sculpting process, as shown in Figure 6-30.

My standard acrylic paint pallete for eyes includes:

- gesso,
- black,
- walnut,
- autumn brown,
- raw sienna,

Figure 6-30 *The dog, created by Ford Bentley, a student at The Art Institute of Phoenix, had its eyes painted with acrylic paints.*

- tomato spice,
- red iron oxide, and
- burnt umber.

Additional colors can be used for iris color. In this exercise, autumn brown will be used as the iris color.

The paint palette is placed on palette paper so it is easily discarded. The brushes I use for eyes are as fine as I can get. They're called "spotters" and can be found as small as 18-ott size. If you can't find brushes small enough, you can pull hairs from a slightly larger brush until it is the size you desire.

Now let's paint the eyes:

1. Mix gesso, water, and a small amount of raw sienna to make a yellow-tinged whitewash. Never use stark white on the whites of the eyes. Eye whites tinged yellow or blue have a more realistic look.

2. Using a small-tipped brush, paint the sclera (white) of the eye carefully.

   Use a hair dryer to dry the paint before the next step.

3. Add water to the mix and paint a second coat. Dry again and repeat. Always use several thin coats instead of one or two thick coats so the paint will dry evenly.

4. Make a thin wash of raw sienna and water. Outline the inside of the eye along the lids to add shadow and make the eye appear more spherical.

5. Add some red iron oxide to the above mixture and paint the tear duct area at the inner corner of the eye. Continue that color down along the bottom lid.

6. Add burnt umber to the mix and paint a thin line along the top inner lid to produce more shadow.

Now it's time to place the color of the eye.

TIP

MAKING HIGH-LIGHT LIGHTER

If you want the highlight to be lighter, add a little gesso to the paint. Don't use much, though; it will muddy up the look.

1. Using burnt umber without water, load the end of your brush.
2. Make a dot in the center of the eye, making sure that the dot covers enough of the eyeball for the iris. Remember that the eyelids will cover the iris on the top and bottom edge.

    Tip: Don't make the eyes stare. Always place the iris a little to the left or right of center, to keep the figure from appearing to stare into space.
3. Dry the paint with the hair dryer.

    Now let's use a lighter shade of brown for the actual iris shade of the eye.

1. Use autumn brown and make a dot inside the first one you placed in the eye, making sure you leave just a slight edge of dark color surrounding the lighter one.
2. Dry the paint with the hair dryer again.

    Now we'll place the pupil in the eye.

1. Use black paint to form the pupil in the center of the eye.
2. Dry the paint again.
3. Mix raw sienna and water, and paint the lighter-brown shade of the eye color with the raw-sienna mixture to highlight one side of the eye.

    When repeating this step for the other eye, make sure it's highlighted on the same side as the other eye.

    Now we'll add light coming into the eye.

1. Decide which side the light will be coming into the eye from.
2. Drag a small amount of gesso from just into the pupil out. This should only be a very small amount.

    When adding light to the other eye, make sure it is placed on the same side of the eye.
3. In the white of the eye along the edge of the iris, add a small amount of gesso. This makes the eye look more rounded.

    To give the eyes a wet look, Liquitex gloss medium and varnish can be applied.

Painting Hair

Now that the eyes are painted, we can paint the eyebrows, mustaches, beards, or hair. When painting hair, keep the following in mind:

*   Hair is never all one color, as seen in Figure 6-31. There are many color variants and shadows that give hair a natural look.
*   When painting eyebrows or any hair that will show individual hairs, paint layers of colors, stroking hairs on the surface as you paint.
*   Painting hair on the head can depend on the style in which you're sculpting the piece. Usually you've sculpted in the strands, so paint the colors and then wash with a darker shadow paint. Wipe off any excess.

Figure 6-31 *Sabrina Bogan, a student at The Art Institute of Phoenix, has added many colors to her sculpture of the little boy with bunny slippers.*

Painting Spots

Freckles, age spots, or whatever spots you want to add to the skin of your creation can be added without making the character look as if it has broken out in polka dots. If you have old brushes that have many mashed and bent hairs, use these to produce spotty patterns that look natural. However, most of us don't have the perfect old brush for our needs. I found that simply taking a small brush and dotting paint on the surface of the skin left a lot to be desired. Now, when I need age spots, freckles, or just a spotted pattern on the skin, I dot the spots on my fingertip and then use my finger to dot over the surface of the skin. The more you dot with your finger, the more shades of the spots appear on the skin so they don't appear as a pattern on the surface. (See Figure 6-32.)

Figure 6-32 *This magnificent character by Richard and Jodi Creager shows age spots artfully applied to the face and hands.*

The Final Finish

The final step is to spray the sculpture with a matte finish. This will keep the surface paint from rubbing off and protect it from the elements. I use Krylon matte finish spray #1311.

1. Hold the clay head out at arm's length and spray the head lightly with the Krylon matte finish spray. Make sure you only run the head through the mist. Spraying too close or too long produces an over-shiny, plastic finish. No matte spray is truly matte when sprayed close up.

2. Let the spray dry thoroughly and repeat two more times. Each time, diminish the amount of spraying until, for the final spray, you simply spray the finish in the air and run the head through the mist.

Using Fiber Hair

If you want a more lifelike look for your character's hair, you might try fiber hair. I use many different types of fiber, depending on the type of character I'm creating. Sheep's fleece, mohair, silk, and synthetic materials are useful. These fibers produce a textured look and give the character a more lively appearance.

Sheep's Fleece

Sheep's fleece is my fiber of choice for most human-type hair. It comes in many colors, and in many different lengths, coarseness, and curl. It can be used raw from the sheep after it's been cleaned; or carded (combed) to take out the natural wave and shininess and to produce a more frizzed appearance. It can be purchased from sheep growers, spinners, and weavers all over the country either as raw cut fleece or as skins.

Sheep varieties such as Cottswold have long, luxurious coats that work well for hair. New Zealand sheep also have beautiful long fleece; it can be purchased as skins.

Using Fleece or Skins
Shorn Fleece

Using shorn fleece is more humane in some people's opinion, and is quite suitable for the purpose. However, it can be a challenge to lay out the pieces of fiber you will eventually be piecing together on the character's head so that the final hairstyle lies the way you envisioned it.

I use medium to thick cyanoacrylate (super glue) for attachment of the hair to the clay head.

Here are some tips to remember when applying shorn fiber:

- Draw a plan of how the hair will lie on the head.
- Glue hair along the hairline first, making sure it lies in the appropriate direction.

- Glue hair for the front hairline and parts in the opposite direction to the one in which it will lie, allowing the hair to be brought back over the glued edge and hide it from sight.

- Continue gluing hair in the direction it lies as you work your way to the back of the head.

- If you add a ponytail or bun on the character's head, excess fibers can be used to fill spaces under the hair to hide the scalp.

Note: For another approach to applying hair to your character, see Antonette Cely's Web site, listed in the Appendix under Artists.

Skins

Skins can also be used for hair or fur. Skins have a great advantage over shorn fleece in that they can give the illusion of rooted hair.

Here are some tips to remember when applying skins:

- Always check the skin side to see where the skin (or leather) is thinner. The thinner the leather, the easier it will be to hide edges and manipulate the piece.

- Skins should be cut from the leather side only. Use an X-acto knife to cut through the skin only, not the fur. The skin can then be pulled apart, leaving the fur intact around the edges.

- A pattern can be drawn on a paper towel to match the size and shape of the head. Paper towel is my choice of pattern paper because it is soft and it drapes, but it still resists to tearing.

- To hide the edge of the leather around the hairline, incise the hairline around the clay head and shell out the back of the head the depth of the leather thickness. This allows the leather to sit down into the head when it's applied, hiding the raw edge.

- Comb the hair to remove excess if it's too bushy.

- Skins can be applied with cyanoacrylate, but be careful not to get any on the hairline where it would show.

Silk and Synthetic Fiber

There are many synthetic fibers that work well for maquettes. I also use silk thread to produce straight, long hair for characters that require this look. Working with threads, strings, and ropes of different types introduces a new range of problems.

Here are some tips to remember when using silk and other synthetic fibers:

1. Using a piece of cardboard as wide as the hair will be long, wrap the thread around the cardboard until a sufficient bundle has been wound.

2. Tie the wound hair with a separate piece of thread at one side, and slide the bundle off the cardboard.

3. Cut the opposite side of the loop from the tied string. Now you have straight hair hanging down, tied together by the thread.

Follow the same instructions for shorn fleece above to secure it to the head. You can make as many bundles of hair as you need to cover the character's head.

Human Hair

I do not recommend using human hair for maquettes, because it is extremely hard to work with. The shinny, slippery surface is attractive but impractical. Just holding onto it while trying to attach it to the head can be quite frustrating.

Readymade Wigs

Some people use readymade wigs found in doll shops and stores. I don't recommend these, as the heads you create will not be a standard size or shape. The wigs tend to be too large and out-of-scale compared to the rest of the character. Creating your own hair is more likely to result in hair that looks like it was grown on your character, rather than a bad hairpiece that was added as an afterthought.

Fabric Clothing

If you want fabric clothing for your character, you must have a plan and patience. Remember that this isn't like dressing Barbie and GI Joe. The character is static, meaning that the arms and legs won't move to allow easy access for sleeves and pant legs. Also, fabric and clothing styles need to be made to scale to fit the rest of the character.

Clothes are typically built right on the character. This allows for fewer layers of bulky material and also lets you create the outfit systematically.

Here are some tips to remember when creating clothes from fabric:

- Use fabric glue instead of sewing the fabric. It creates a stronger bond and less bulky seams.
- Apply clothes in layers, only adding parts that will show. In other words, if the character is wearing a sweater and coat, only the front of the sweater need be applied under the coat if you will never see the rest of the sweater.
- Make everything by hand. Store-bought objects are rarely to scale and very often stand out because they are created in a different style than your character. Exceptions to this rule are items like baby socks and sweaters used for socks and sweaters on the characters.

Creating Leather Shoes

Shoes and boots are always popular items to make. They can give a character that real, finished look. I use old glove leather for my shoes because it's very thin and malleable. Belt leather is my choice for soles, especially if I have an armature wire coming down through the foot into a base. The holes in the belt work great for allowing the wire through without my having to punch a hole in the leather myself.

The shoes are planned out just as any other piece of clothing is. Because the character's feet will be different sizes, a pattern must be made for each foot. I start by drawing a pattern around the circumference of the foot. This gives me a close outline for the sole. Then, using my handy paper towel, I cut a slit in the towel and place it over the top of the foot brining the slit around the ankle. Now I can trace around the foot to get the size and shape I need for the top of the shoe. If the shoe has side panels and tongues, maybe a lace-up front, I check the pieces of leather I have. Most gloves have pre-sewn edges that can be used on the shoe. I create a pattern for each piece. When the shoe is pieced together on the foot, the edges of the leather for the top portions are brought around to the underside of the foot where they are glued securely. Any raw edges of the leather that still show can be covered with braid or small decorative trim. The sole is glued on last, to cover all raw and glued edges. Boot tops can be applied in the same fashion.

In Conclusion

Now we've gone from start to finish and created a maquette character. The approach isn't unique nor is it the only approach to use. This is only a starting point for you. Try everything. Learn as much as you can and make your own judgments about what works for you. This is a creative endeavor that is limited only by your imagination.

In the Next Chapter

In Chapter 7 we will explore the use of digitizing equipment to turn clay characters into computer models.

Chapter 7
Digitizing

Chapter Objectives

- Learn about digitizers.
- Learn to build digitizing models.
- Learn to use laser scanners.
- Learn to build laser scan models.

In Chapters 2 through 6, we covered the design and creation of a maquette clay model of a character. Now it's time to talk about other areas of character creation with clay.

Maquettes are used as reference tools for animators and artists. But what if you need your character to be animated in a computer? If you've ever tried modeling realistic human characters in a 3D modeling program, you know how difficult it can be to get the results you want.

Creating computer-generated characters is one of the animation industry's most challenging arts. Even with the incredible advances in computer power, it's still a difficult task to create credible, enjoyable characters completely in a computer environment. Recent advances in software design and hardware power have led to such successes as the greedy toy collector in Pixar's *Toy Story 2* and the leading "man" in Columbia Tristar's *Stuart Little*. These characters both began as clay models, which were then digitized into a computer. This solution cuts the time required to construct functional characters, while increasing their quality and usability.

Digitizing is the process of converting points on the surface of a model into a spatially accurate representation of them in the mathematical world of the computer. Each point on the model equates to a point in 3D space in the computer. Those 3D points are then used to create a surface that can be viewed and manipulated. The computer artist can assign a color and other surface characteristics, such as shininess, roughness, and opacity. The artist can also add hair or fur and control how the character moves and looks.

There are several methods commonly used to digitize objects into the computer. The two most popular are manual touch-probe devices called *digitizing arms* and the faster *laser scanners.* Both create a web of points in 3D space, but each technology has its own strengths and limitations, as we learned in Chapter 3.

Digitizing Arms

Digitizing arms, as seen in Figure 7-1, are used extensively in creating computer models.

Figure 7-1 *Digitizing arms from Immersion are used to digitize clay models into the computer.*

They range from small and relatively inexpensive ($2,000) tabletop models to large and expensive models used to digitize entire motorcycles, for example. The arm itself is mechanically linked to allow smooth, accurate, repeatable motion in 6 degrees of freedom with an accuracy greater than two hundredths of an inch. Electrical controls at all joints produce signals that are combined to represent the position of the tip at a point in space. When the tip is properly positioned, as shown in Figure 7-2, the operator presses a switch to transmit this position to the computer.

This can be a quite laborious process, as the arm tip must be placed carefully on each point on the model's surface and held while the position signal is generated. In spite of the painstaking nature of this process, however, it's still quicker than modeling in the computer and usually produces better results as well.

The arm base and model must be fixed onto a surface near the computer so that the model and arm maintain a fixed relationship during the digitizing process. If either moves, the accuracy of the process is compromised and the process must then be repeated. The arm is connected to the computer via a ser-

Figure 7-2 *The digitizing tip is held in position on the model to produce a duplicate point in 3D space on the computer.*

ial cable. A foot switch is usually used to keep the hands free while the digitizing process is under way. A compatible software package is used to provide an interface with which to work inside the computer. These software packages are available from the arm manufacturers as well as from third parties.

The Digitizing Model

A digitizing model differs from a maquette in numerous ways. The first difference is in the position in which a digitizing model is created. Unlike a maquette that is typically modeled in an action or character pose, a digitizing model is sculpted in a *reference* or *neutral* position—arms out to the side, looking straight ahead, feet slightly apart. This position is sometimes called the Leonardo da Vinci position because of its similarity to the classic study of proportions shown in Figure 7-3.

This position lets the artist get the digitizing arm tip into the underarms and between the legs to ensure an accurate model in the computer.

Digitizing models don't even have to be sculpted as a single unit. They can—and usually should—be sculpted in parts, so that the portions of the anatomy requiring more detail can be sculpted in a larger scale. Typically, the head and hands are sculpted in a larger scale and the body and legs in a smaller scale. In the computer, it's easy to resize all of these elements and sew the surfaces together to form a smooth whole.

Some digitizing sculptors use Sculpey or Super Sculpey for their models and cure them to form a smooth surface. These clays tend to produce a relatively rough surface that can cause the digitizing point to drag. Because of this, some digitizer sculptors use plastilina or other nonhardening clay because of its smooth surface. Of course, because the surface is never perfectly hard, extreme care must be used to avoid digging the digitizer tip into the clay. One solution is to thor-

Figure 7-3 *Leonardo da Vinci's classic study of proportions.*

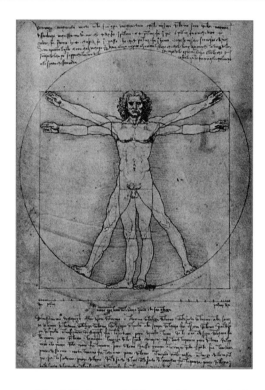

oughly chill the model in a refrigerator before digitizing; the result is a smooth and relatively hard surface—but rather chilly to work on! Another solution to this problem is to make a mold from the plastilina model and cast it in resin.

After the model has been sculpted, the digitizer operator draws a grid on the surface of the model, as shown in Figure 7-4. This grid allows the artist to visualize where the points in 3D space are positioned and to ensure complete and even coverage of the model.

Figure 7-4 *The digitizing model built for the aliens in the movie* The Arrival *has a grid drawn on its surface for digitizing points into 3D space.*

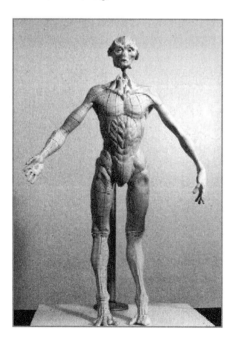

Note: If the character is symmetrical, only one side needs a grid. The structure can be mirrored in the computer, making the one-half model into a whole.

The more complex the surface is on your model, the more grid lines you'll need in that area so the resulting mesh object is complex enough to show adequate detail. On the other hand, areas of little detail, like the back of a head, require very few grid lines to define the smooth surface.

The digitizing model must be secured to a base that provides freedom of movement around the model without letting the base move from its position. A turntable can be used as long as the turntable base is secured so it does not move along any of the three axes (X, Y, and Z) while digitizing.

X—Right to left

Y—Up and down

Z—In and out

Digitizing the Model

Before beginning to digitize the character, a reference point for each of the three axes must be determined. This just lets you know if something has slipped during the operation that would throw off the computer mesh dimensions.

Following the gridlines on the clay model, the artist places the movable end of the digitizing arm at each grid intersection on the surface of the model and clicks the foot pedal. Depending upon the software, the artist might also keep the tip in contact with the surface and move it smoothly along a grid line, generating a spline curve in the computer. After additional lines are digitized, the curves that are generated form a duplicate of the surface characteristics in 3D space in the computer, as shown in Figure 7-5.

Figure 7-5 *The digitized computer model is shown as spline curves.*

Immersion Corporation is a leader in digitizing arms. The company has developed a mechanical tracking technology with a unique and attractive mechanical arm that is compact, affordable, and easy to use. The MicroScribe-3D arm combines graphite links for a lightweight yet rugged structure and precision bearings for smooth, almost effortless manipulation. Each joint uses digital optical sensors, which are immune from any environmental noise and interference. The result is a versatile system that can work in almost any environment and be used with objects of any material. With accuracy of up to 0.009 mm and sampling speeds of up to 1,000 Hz, MicroScribe-3D is truly the ultimate 3D digitizing system.

Advantages of Using a Digitizing Arm

- The arms come in small sizes for low cost and portability of the units.
- Scanning is user-controlled.
- Results are relatively accurate (+0.02mm).
- No problems are encountered with undercuts (under chins, noses, under arms, and so on).

Disadvantages of Using a Digitizing Arm

- The surface must be hard enough so that it doesn't give as you run the tip of the arm on it. Soft rubber certainly would not work well for this.
- The more complex the surface, the more time-intensive the operation.
- The arm size limits the size of the model you can use.
- Slight movements of either the arm base or the model can throw off the accuracy of the computer-generated mesh.

Laser Scanners

Although digitizing arms are very good at duplicating clay models in computer space, they can be time-consuming and inaccurate and there is a limit to the model size that can be digitized. To answer the industry's need for digitizing larger models faster and with more accuracy, laser scan technology, long used for engineering and medical diagnostic imaging, provides an alternative.

The 3D laser scanners differ from digitizing arms in that they are automatic machines that use laser lights bounced off the external surface of an object and reflected onto sensors, rather than the manual touch-probe arm device, as shown in Figure 7-6.

No grid is required on the surface of these models, as the scanner works by casting a fan or stripe of laser light over the object, while cameras view the laser from either side to record cross-sectional profiles of the object. A magnetic tracker is used to determine position and orientation, enabling the computer to reconstruct the full three-dimensional surface of the object. The advantage to this method is that the model never comes in contact with the device, making it easy to use any substance for the model. The laser beam scans the object on several planes and the resulting geometric data produces a "point cloud" representation of the object in the computer. This makes it much easier to replicate non-symmetrical models.

Figure 7-6 *The large laser scanner shown is a product of Digibotics, courtesy of NVision. It is their largest and can scan objects up to 36" in diameter and 6 feet in height. Notice that it has no mechanical arm, but scans the surface with a laser beam. For other laser scanning devices, see NVision in the Appendix.*

Although laser scanners are a much faster method of digitizing a model initially, they can be much more time consuming at the other end when all the "point cloud" data has to be cleaned up to form a useable model.

Size is also a consideration. Standard laser scanners are large, static machines that rotate either the model or the laser beam itself to gather the needed data. This has effectively taken the technology out of the hands of amateur and freelance sculptors and animators. Even some of the large animation houses such as PDI (who created the hit 3D animated movie *Antz*) send their clay models out-of-house to be digitized.

New "portable" laser scanners are being created and might well be the answer to future digitizing problems. NVision, a Dallas, Texas company, advertises a handheld scanner that is as small as a desktop digitizing arm. Polhemus, Inc. in Vermont, known for its 3D position and orientation tracking, motion capture, and digitizing technology, also advertises a handheld scanner. These smaller scanners offer the same freedom as a digital arm, but are faster and more accurate. Since some of the scanners boast the ability to create from 7,000 to 15,000 points per second on the surface of the computer model, you can see that this technology speeds up the digitizing process.

Creating a Laser Scan Model

Creating a digitizing model to be scanned is similar to creating one to be digitized with an arm. However, because the scanner never physically touches the surface of the model, the model can be constructed of many different substances. From squishy to fragile, the model's surface is largely inconsequential,

Figure 7-7 *Michael Jordon has been scanned with a Digibot laser scanner to create this computer replica.*

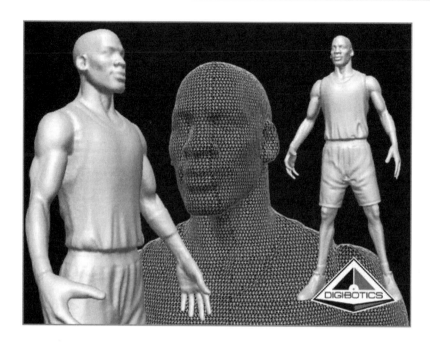

as no mechanical device will actually come in contact with the piece. However, it is important to note that most scanners are designed to work on nonmetallic, opaque objects. Because scanning relies on the camera seeing the laser line, some surfaces may not be suitable for laser scanning, such as translucent, reflective, dark, or deeply convoluted surfaces.

The versatility of the laser scanner is evident from the ease with which it can scan a human face to produce a computer generated "life mask." This technique is common in the movie industry to generate digital stand-ins for human actors. See Figure 7-7 for an example of laser scanning of a human subject.

Scanning the Model

Unlike the digitizing model used with a digitizing arm, it can sometimes be a problem to scan a model as a whole. Because the laser scanner surveys the outer skin of the object, concave areas under the arms, nose, and chin and between the legs are sometimes missed. Some artists have gotten around this, as you read in the interviews in Chapter 3, by cutting their clay models apart so that a single arm or leg can be scanned separately from the torso.

After an object has been digitized, the data can be exported in the form of IGES polylines or splines; STL and DXF polygon meshes; or XYZ points; the output is then ready for importing directly into the computer modeling program.

Operation of a scanner in the presence of metal objects or electromagnetic fields may interfere with the scanner's tracking and degrade its performance. Another common problem with laser scanners is that they commonly produce unnecessarily dense meshes that are often unacceptable for animators, engineers, game developers, designers, and other users who require more manageable surface features and data file sizes. While the laser scanning process itself is quick, the post-processing required to turn the automatically generated data into an acceptable computer image can be time-consuming and expensive.

Advantages of Using Laser Scanners

- They have high accuracy for higher surface detail (±0.001mm).
- They are fast—15,000 points per second or more.
- They can reproduce texture mapping simultaneously with the scan.
- They can scan much larger models.

Disadvantages of Using Laser Scanners

- They are very expensive and usually relatively large floor units.
- They automatically create very dense meshes.
- They don't work well on reflective and transparent surfaces.
- They do not scan undercuts well.

In Conclusion

We've seen the future, and it's digital. But even digital magic can't replace the tactile touch and feel of traditional character building. Clay and artists won't be replaced by a computer any time soon. Wonderful creations can still be born from a ball of clay in your hand.

Appendix

Resources

Animation Sites

Pixar
http://www.pixar.com/

Stop Motion Animation
Everything you want to know about stop-motion animation.
http://www.stopmotionanimation.com/

Wallace and Gromit
http://www.aardman.com/wallaceandgromit/index.shtml

Armatures

ARMAVERSE
211 N. Union Street
Westfield, IN 46074
Manufactures and sells armature kits and parts with precision-stamped stainless steel plates and anodized steel one-piece ball joints.
http://www.armaverse.com/

EFFECTive ENGINEERING
9932 Mesa Rim Road, Suite B
San Diego, CA 92121
EFFECTive ENGINEERING is the source for cost-effective animatronics and accessories for costumes and creatures.
http://www.effecteng.com/

Gryphyn
716 Halifax Rd. Eastwood
Todmorden, Lancs. OL14 6DP. UK
Phone: 01706 818863
High-end armature manufacturer.
http://easyweb.easynet.co.uk/edawe/index.htm

Meritex Inc.
5101 San Leandro St.
Oakland, CA 94601
510-534-9018
Fax: 510-534-3372
Supplier of all types of armature parts, ball joints, etc.
http://www.jkcamera.com/puppet_animation.htm

Small Parts Inc.
13980 NW 58th Ct.
PO Box 4650
Miami Lakes, FL 33014-0650

Special Shapes
PO Box 7487
Romeoville, IL 60446
Fax: 630-759-1978
Phone: 630-759-1970
Sells all types of brass shapes: bars, tubing, screws, tools, and miscellaneous.
http://www.specialshapes.com/index.htm

Artist Sites

Antonette Cely
Many character figures, with hints and tips on adding hair to your character.
http://www.cely.com/doll.html

Creager Doll Studio
Wonderful character sculptors. Videos and seminars available.
www.creagers.com

June Goodnow
Specialty in ethnic characters. Seminar and videos available.
http://members.aol.com/junedolls/index.html

The George Stuart Historical Figures
See George Stuart's incredible historical characters.
http://members.aol.com/gsfigures/index.html

Clays

Accent Import-Export, Inc.
1501 Loveridge Rd. Box 16
Pittsburg, CA 94565
Phone: 925-431-1150
Fax: 925-431-1152
Importers of Fimo Clay.
http://www.fimozone.com/

Burman Industries
14141 Covello Street, Suite 10-C
VanNuys, CA 91405
(818) 782-9833
Sells a variety of clays, tools, and casting products. On-line catalog and ordering available.
http://www.burmanfoam.com/

Chavant, Inc.
42 West Street
Red Bank, NJ 07701
Phone: (732) 842-6272
Toll Free (USA only): 1-800-CHAVANT (800)-242-8268
Fax: (732) 842-3621
E-mail: *Mail@chavant.com*

Manufactures Chevant modeling clays.
http://www.chavant.com/

Clay Factory of Escondido
750 N. Citracado Pkwy #21
Escondido, CA 92029
Mailing address
PO Box 460598
Escondido, CA 92046-0598
1-877-SCULPEY (728-5739)
Supplier of Cernit clay, Sculpey products, tools, and wire.
http://www.clayfactory.net/

Creative Paperclay
79 Daily Dr., Suite 101
Camarillo, CA 93010
(805) 484-6648
Manufactures Paperclay.
http://www.paperclay.com/

Polyform Products Co.
1901 Estes
Elk Grove Village, IL 60007
Manufactures Sculpey, Super Sculpey, Premo, Sculpey III, and Super Flex clays.
http://www.sculpey.com/fset_products.htm

Digitizing

NVision 3D
1400 Turtle Creek Blvd.
Suite 209
Dallas, TX 75207
Phone: 214-752-0008
Fax: 214-752-0018
A great source for digitizing services and equipment.
http://www.nvision3d.com/news.html

Immersion Corporation
2158 Paragon Drive
San Jose, California 95131
Phone: 408-467-1900
Fax: 408-467-1901
A great source for the Microscibe Digitizing arm and touch sense devices.
http://www.immerse.com/contact.html

Glass and Plastic Eyes

EZ Pose Flexible Doll Bodies
PO Box 97
Crestone, CO 81131
Phone: 719-256-4235
Fax: 719-256-420
Supplier of porcelain eyes, armature parts, and clays.
http://www.ezpose.com/supplies.html

Latex and Resin Casting

The Monster Makers
7305 Detroit Ave.
Cleveland, OH 44102
Tel: 216-651-SPFX (7739)
Fax: 216-631-4FAX (4329)
Supplies latex foam kits, videos, and tools.
http://www.monstermakers.com

Tom Banwell Designs
PO Box 361
Penn Valley, CA 95946
Phone: 530-432-1464
Fax: 530-432-5302
Offers resin casting products and seminars.
http://www.lumicast.com/

Publications

Amazing Figure Modeler Magazine
Discover the exciting world of horror, science fiction, and fantasy figure modeling.
http://www.amazingmodeler.com/

Cinefex Magazine
The premier magazine on specal effects in the entertainment industry.
http://visualeffects.net/effectsguide/cinefex/Cinefexcontents.html

Sheep Fleece, Skins, and Leather

Golden Fleece Wool Processing and Sales
260 Oak St.
Goldendale, WA 98620
(509) 773-6122
Fax: (509) 773-4630
E-mail: *goldenfleece@gorge.net*
Various types of raw and carded fleece.

Guenhwyvar's Antique Spinning Wheels & Fiber
7765 Forest Ridge Dr.
Bremerton, WA 98311
http://www.webspawner.com/users/guenhwyvar/
Various types of raw and carded wools, mohair, angora, etc.

Southforty Farms
34184 Quail Creek Lane
Wildomar, CA 92595
(909) 471-2992 (9am–4pm Mon–Fri., Pacific Time)
Fax: (413) 480-2411
Great supplier of fleece, skins, fur, and leather. Also has videos available on how to make your own skin wigs.
http://www.southfortyfarms.com/

Tandy Leather Co.
120 Brock Street
PO Box 13,000
Barrie, ON
Canada L4M 4W4
1-800-387-9815
1-705-728-2481
Fax: 1-705-721-1226
Supplier of leathers, craft supplies, and tools.
http://www.tandyleather.ca/

Tongue River Farm
HC40 Broadus Stage
Miles City, MT 59301
Icelandic Sheep Pelts
Beautiful pelts that feel soft and look like fox. Many patterns available with the colors of black, white, and moorit.
http://www.icelandicsheep.com/

Yellow Wool Llamas
Fred and Laura Keller
1095 Observatory Road
Martinsville, IN 46151
317-834-9097
http://www.ywl.com/wool/fleece.htm
Supplier of yellow llama fleece and wool.

Tools

Micro Mark
340 Snyder Avenue (rear entrance)
Berkeley Heights, NJ
Distributor of hard-to-find small tools.
On-line catalog available.
http://www.micromark.com/store.html

Perfect Touch
24 Artesia
Conroe, TX 77304-2516
Great wooden sculpting tools.
http://perfect-touch.com/index.htp

Videos

Creager Doll Studios
A great Web site to see Richard and Jodi Creager's beautiful characters. They also offer instructional videos on sculpting the head and hands, which I highly recommend.
http://creagers.com

Mindstorm Productions
Distributes various videos on sculpting.
http://perfect-touch.com/index.htp

Glossary

Animatronics—Animated puppets using either electronic or mechanical means.

Armature—Wire skeleton giving the maquette its form.

Burnishing—Creating a glass-like finish on clay by rubbing with a smooth polished stone.

Carpal bones—Bones of the wrist.

Cernit—A polymer clay manufactired by T+F GmbH, Dreieich, Germany. It can be either baked in an oven or boiled.

Chavant—A line of plastilina-type clays created for industrial use. Come in many different hardnesses.

Clavicular notch—Also called the "pit" of the neck, where the sternum (breastbone) and clavicle (collarbone) come together.

Claymation—Term coined by stop-motion animator Wil Vinton for stop-motion animation with clay characters.

Concept drawing—A preliminary drawing showing ideas of how a character might look.

Cyanacrylic glue—Fast-drying "instant" glue such as Super Glue or Crazy Glue.

Da Vinci position—*See* Reference Pose.

Dental spoon—A dental instrument with a rounded, spoon-like end.

Digitizing—The process of converting points on the surface of a model into a spatially accurate representation of them in the mathematical world of the computer.

Digitizing arm—A mechanical device used in conjunction with a computer to replicate a clay sculpture into a computer-generated model.

Digitizing model—Sculpted clay model used to replicate the surface into a computer by use of either a digitizing arm or laser scanner.

Earth clay—An earthy material that is plastic when moist but hard when fired, composed mainly of fine particles of hydrous aluminum silicates and other minerals, and that is used for making brick, tile, and pottery.

Epicanthic fold—A fold in the Asian eye that overlaps the lower lid slightly at the tear duct and also may overlap the lower lid at the outer corner of the eye.

Epoxy glue—A resin-based, two-part glue that has to be mixed prior to using.

Fimo—A polymer, oil-based clay from Eberhard Faber in Germany. Similar to Sculpey III.

Finger rest—A pad of clay placed at the back of the head to rest finger on while sculpting.

Firing—Hardening the clay with heat.

Grid line—Crosshatch lines drawn on the surface of a digitizing model to show where computer-generated splines will be made.

Hot-melt glue—Hot glue used in sticks with a hot glue gun.

Kleen Klay—A plastilina-type clay.

Laser scanner—Uses laser light to scan the clay model surface and replicate it into a computer-generated model.

Lava soap—Brand name for a soap containing pumice.

Life mask—An exact copy of a face made with either a mold or a laser scanner.

Maquette—A 12- to 18-inch clay model used for reference. Uusally sculpted in an action pose.

Matte finish spray—A non-glossy acrylic clear spray used to seal finishes.

Metacarpal bones—Bones of the hands.

Metatarsal bones—Bones of the feet.

Model sheet—Drawings of a character in front, side, and three-quarter views and action poses. Sometimes include facial expressions.

Nasiolabial fold—Fold or furrow that runs from the side of the nose down alongside the mouth to the jowls.

Obicularis-oculi—The muscle that narrows the eye.

Orange stick—A manicure or spa stick to care for cuticles. Can be found in beauty supply stores.

Oven-baked clay—Clay that is fired at low temperatures in an oven until hardened.

Paperclay—A papier-mache-type clay that is an air-dry alternative to Super Sculpey.

Papier mache—An air-dried claylike substance created by mixing paper pulp and water.

Phalanges—Bones of the fingers.

Philtrum—Indented fold that runs between the nose and the top edge of the upper lip.

Plasticene—*See* Plastilina.

Plastilina—(aka plasticene) Clay powder mixed with oil and wax instead of water; it comes in many varieties and hardness levels.

Plumber's putty—A resin-based, two-part putty that has to be mixed before using.

Point cloud—Computer geometric data resulting from a laser scan of an object.

Polymer clay—A clay first developed in Germany in 1930. It is made from polyvinyl chloride (PVC).

Premo—Created to replace ProMat. It can be used to blend with Super Sculpey to make it more durable. Not intended to be used on its own.

ProMat—Synthetic clay that is stiffer and harder to work with than Super Sculpey, but will bake harder and take more abuse. Can be mixed with Super Sculpey.

Reference pose—aka "da Vinci" position. Used for digitizing and computer models. Arms out to the side, looking straight ahead, feet slightly apart.

Roma plastilina—Synthetic clay that comes in four softness ranges (1-4).

Schematic drawing—Drawing to scale of a character. Usually only front and side views.

Sculpey—A white polymer clay from Polyform Products, rougher in texture after firing and more difficult to sculpt with its soft consistency than some other polymer clays. Super Sculpey has generally replaced it.

Sculpey III—Similar to Super Sculpey but is usually sold in smaller quantities. It comes in a variety of colors.

Sculpey diluent—Oil-based liquid manufactured by Polyform Products to soften Super Sculpey.

Sculpting stand—Wooden armature and base used to hold a sculpture while working.

Shoulder plate—Sculpted area that includes the neck, shoulders, and chest area and that lies on and can be attached to a cloth body.

Spline curve—The computer-generated line along a model's surface. When all splines are stitched together, they form the final form.

Sterno-mastoid muscles—The two muscles that have the most to do with the look of the neck. They come up from the sternum (or breastbone) to below and in back of the ears (mastoid).

Stop-motion—The cinematic process by which a posable puppet is brought to life on screen by filming slight movements one frame at a time. When the final film is projected, the puppet appears to move of its own volition.

Super Sculpey—Synthetic oil-based clay that can be fired in a standard home oven at relatively low temperatures. It has a pink skin tone, a smoother texture than Sculpey, and is much easier to sculpt. It is the most popular clay for sculpting smaller maquettes.

Synthetic clay—Clays made from polyvinyl chloride (PVC).

Tarsal bones—Bones of the ankles.

Tragus—The little cartilage lump that protrudes into the bowl area of the ear from the front.

Trapizius muscles—Cape-like shoulder muscles that come up and attach to the base of the skull.

Tubercle—A slight protuberance in the middle of the upper lip.

Wattle—Area of sagging skin under the chin area.

Wed clay—A water-based clay that dries very slowly and has many of the same sculpting qualities as oil clay. Excellent for large, detailed sculptures. Requires the use of a spray bottle of water to maintain moistness. Brown in color.

Wet-dry sandpaper—Sandpaper that can be used with or without water.

Zygomatic major—Muscle that pulls on the mouth and, along with the obicularis oculi, creates a smile.

Index

See also the Glossary starting on page 195.